Microsoft® FrontPage® 2000
Brief Edition

INTERACTIVE COMPUTING SERIES

Kenneth C. Laudon
Jason Eiseman

Azimuth Interactive, Inc.

Boston   Burr Ridge, IL   Dubuque, IA   Madison, WI   New York   San Francisco   St. Louis
Bangkok   Bogotá   Caracas   Lisbon   London   Madrid   Mexico City   Milan   New Delhi   Seoul
Singapore   Sydney   Taipei   Toronto

McGraw-Hill Higher Education
A Division of The **McGraw-Hill** Companies

MICROSOFT FRONTPAGE 2000 BRIEF EDITION

Copyright © 2000 by The McGraw-Hill Companies, Inc. All rights reserved. Printed in the United States of America. Except as permitted under the United States Copyright Act of 1976, no part of this publication may be reproduced or distributed in any form or by any means, or stored in a data base or retrieval system, without the prior written permission of the publisher.

 This book is printed on recycled, acid-free paper containing 10% postconsumer waste.

1 2 3 4 5 6 7 8 9 0 QPD/QPD 9 0 9 8 7 6 5 4 3 2 1 0 9

ISBN 0-07-235855-6

Vice president/Editor-in-Chief: *Michael W. Junior*
Publisher: *David Kendric Brake*
Sponsoring editor: *Trisha O'Shea*
Associate Editors: *Scott M. Hamilton/Steve Schuetz*
Developmental editor: *Erin Riley*
Senior marketing manager: *Jeff Parr*
Project manager: *Carrie Sestak*
Production supervisor: *Michael R. McCormick*
Freelance design coordinator: *Pam Verros*
Cover Illustration: *Kip Henrie*
Supplement coordinator: *Matthew Perry*
New Media: *Lisa Ramos-Torrescan*
Compositor: *Azimuth Interactive, Inc.*
Typeface: *10/12 Sabon*
Printer: *Quebecor Printing Book Group/Dubuque*

Library of Congress Catalog Card Number: 99-66180

http://www.mhhe.com

Microsoft® FrontPage® 2000
Brief Edition

INTERACTIVE COMPUTING SERIES

Kenneth C. Laudon
Jason Eiseman

Azimuth Interactive, Inc.

At **McGraw-Hill Higher Education**, we publish instructional materials targeted at the higher education market. In an effort to expand the tools of higher learning, we publish texts, lab manuals, study guides, testing materials, software, and multimedia products.

At **Irwin/McGraw-Hill** (a division of McGraw-Hill Higher Education), we realize technology will continue to create new mediums for professors and students to manage resources and communicate information with one another. We strive to provide the most flexible and complete teaching and learning tools available and offer solutions to the changing world of teaching and learning.

Irwin/McGraw-Hill is dedicated to providing the tools necessary for today's instructors and students to navigate the world of Information Technology successfully.

Seminar Series - Irwin/McGraw-Hill's Technology Connection seminar series offered across the country every year, demonstrates the latest technology products and encourages collaboration among teaching professionals.

Osborne/McGraw-Hill - A division of the McGraw-Hill Companies known for its best-selling Internet titles *Harley Hahn's Internet & Web Yellow Pages* and the *Internet Complete Reference*, offers an additional resource for certification and has strategic publishing relationships with corporations such as Corel Corporation and America Online. For more information, visit Osborne at www.osborne.com.

Digital Solutions - Irwin/McGraw-Hill is committed to publishing Digital Solutions. Taking your course online doesn't have to be a solitary venture. Nor does it have to be a difficult one. We offer several solutions, which will let you enjoy all the benefits of having course material online. For more information, visit www.mhhe.com/solutions/index.mhtml.

Packaging Options - For more about our discount options, contact your local Irwin/McGraw-Hill Sales representative at 1-800-338-3987, or visit our Web site at www.mhhe.com/it.

Preface

Interactive Computing Series

Goals/Philosophy

The *Interactive Computing Series* provides you with an illustrated interactive environment for learning software skills using Microsoft Office. The *Interactive Computing Series* is composed of both text and multimedia interactive CD-ROMs. The text and the CD-ROMs are closely coordinated. *It's up to you. You can choose how you want to learn.*

Approach

The *Interactive Computing Series* is the visual interactive way to develop and apply software skills. This skills-based approach coupled with its highly visual, two-page spread design allows the student to focus on a single skill without having to turn the page. A running case study is provided through the text, reinforcing the skills and giving a real-world focus to the learning process.

About the Book

The **Interactive Computing Series** offers *two levels* of instruction. Each level builds upon the previous level.

Brief lab manual - covers the basics of the application, contains two to four chapters.
Introductory lab manual - includes the material in the Brief textbook plus two to four additional chapters. The Introductory lab manuals prepare students for the *Microsoft Office User Specialist Proficiency Exam (MOUS Certification)*.

Each lesson is organized around **Skills**, **Concepts**, and **Steps (Do It!)**.

Each lesson is divided into a number of Skills. Each **Skill** is first explained at the top of the page.
Each **Concept** is a concise description of why the skill is useful and where it is commonly used.
Each **Step (Do It!)** contains the instructions on how to complete the skill.

About the CD-ROM

The CD-ROM provides a unique interactive environment for students where they learn to use software faster and remember it better. The CD-ROM is organized in a similar approach as the text: The **Skill** is defined, the **Concept** is explained in rich multimedia, and the student performs **Steps (Do It!)** within sections called Interactivities. There are at least <u>45 Interactivities per CD-ROM</u>. Some of the features of the CD-ROM are:

Simulated Environment - The Interactive Computing CD-ROM places students in a simulated controlled environment where they can practice and perform the skills of the application software.
Interactive Exercises - The student is asked to demonstrate command of a specific software skill. The student's actions are followed by a digital "TeacherWizard" that provides feedback.
SmartQuizzes - Provide performance-based assessment of the student at the end of each lesson.

Using the Book

In the book, each skill is described in a two-page graphical spread (Figure 1). The left side of the two-page spread describes the skill, the concept, and the steps needed to perform the skill. The right side of the spread uses screen shots to show you how the screen should look at key stages.

Figure 1

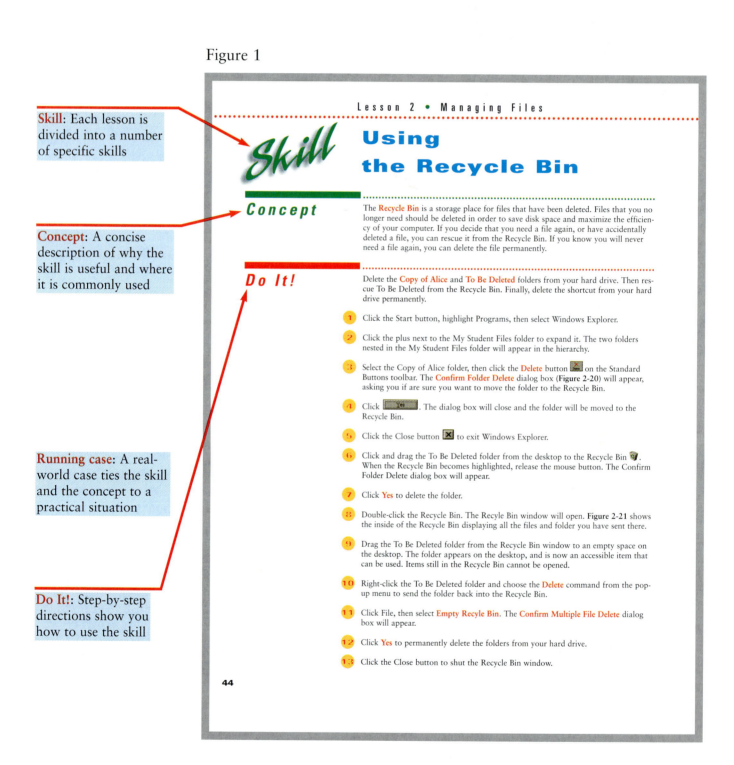

End-of-Lesson Features

In the book, the learning in each lesson is reinforced at the end by a quiz and a skills review called Interactivity, which provides step-by-step exercises and real-world problems for the students to solve independently.

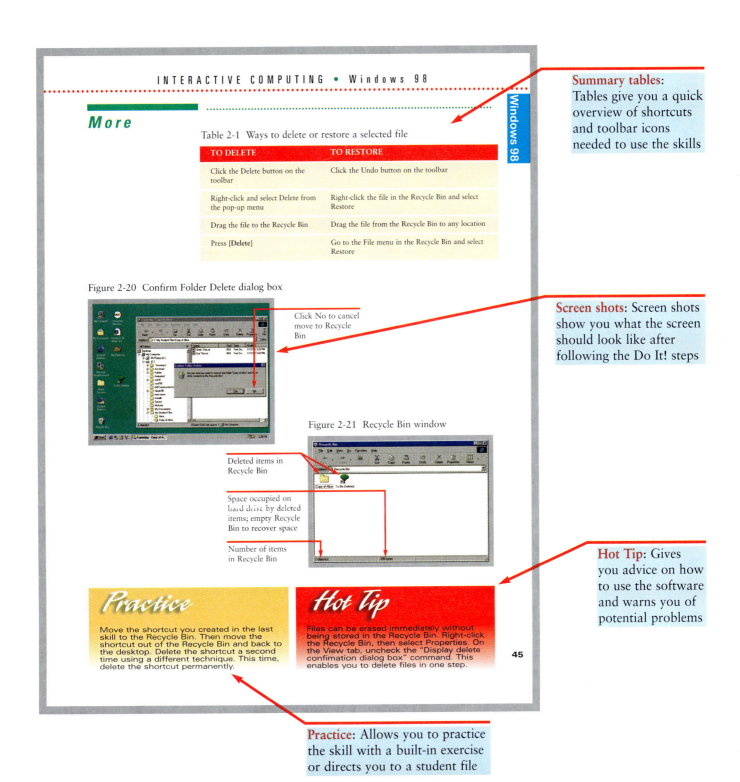

Using the Interactive CD-ROM

The Interactive Computing multimedia CD-ROM provides an unparalleled learning environment in which you can learn software skills faster and better than in books alone. The CD-ROM creates a unique interactive environment in which you can learn to use software faster and remember it better. The CD-ROM uses the same lessons, skills, concepts, and Do It! steps as found in the book, but presents the material using voice, video, animation, and precise simulation of the software you are learning. A typical CD-ROM contents screen shows the major elements of a lesson (see Figure 2 below).

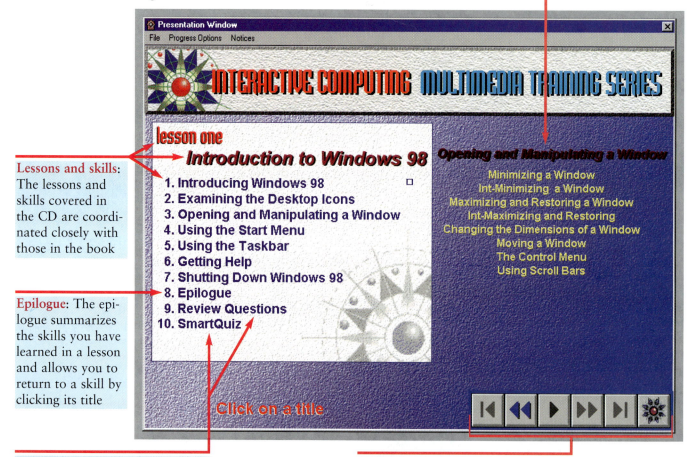

Figure 2

Skills list: A list of skills allows you to jump directly to any skill you want to learn or review, including interactive sessions with the TeacherWizard

Lessons and skills: The lessons and skills covered in the CD are coordinated closely with those in the book

Epilogue: The epilogue summarizes the skills you have learned in a lesson and allows you to return to a skill by clicking its title

Review Questions and **SmartQuiz**: Review Questions test your knowledge of the concepts covered in the lesson; SmartQuiz tests your ability to accomplish tasks in a simulated software environment

User controls: Precise and simple user controls permit you to start, stop, pause, jump forward or backward one sentence, or jump forward or backward an entire skill. A single navigation star takes you back to the lesson's table of contents

Unique Features of the CD-ROM: TeacherWizard™ and SmartQuiz™

Interactive Computing: Software Skills offers many leading-edge features on the CD currently found in no other learning product on the market. One such feature is *interactive exercises* in which you are asked to demonstrate your command of a software skill in a precisely simulated software environment. Your actions are followed closely by a digital TeacherWizard that guides you with additional information if you make a mistake. When you complete the action called for by the TeacherWizard correctly, you are congratulated and prompted to continue the lesson. If you make a mistake, the TeacherWizard gently lets you know: "No, that's not the right icon. Click on the Folder icon on the left side of the top toolbar to open a file." No matter how many mistakes you make, the TeacherWizard is there to help you.

Another leading-edge feature is the end-of-lesson SmartQuiz. Unlike the multiple choice and matching questions found in the book quiz, the SmartQuiz puts you in a simulated digital software world and asks you to show your mastery of skills while actually working with the software (Figure 3).

Figure 3

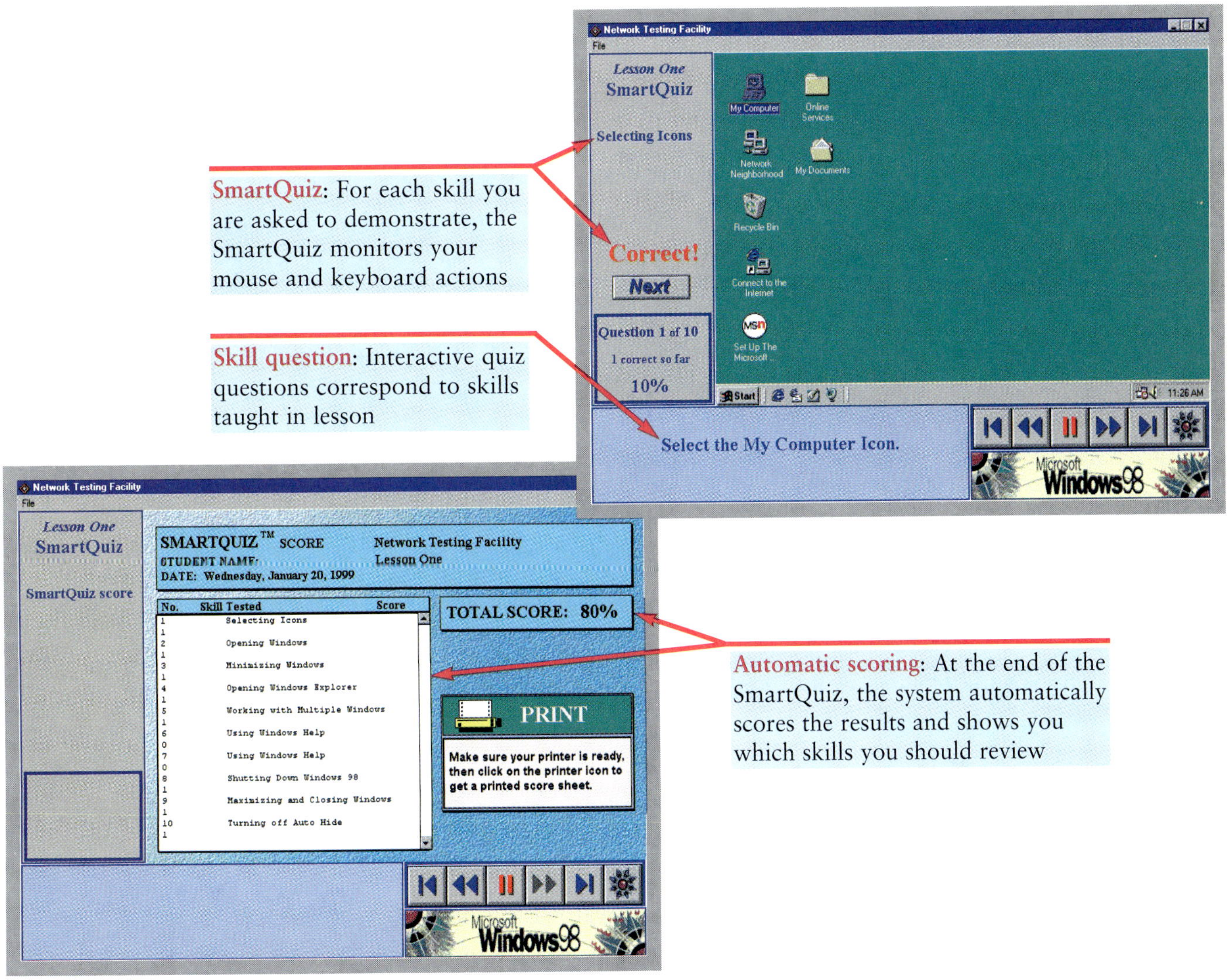

SmartQuiz: For each skill you are asked to demonstrate, the SmartQuiz monitors your mouse and keyboard actions

Skill question: Interactive quiz questions correspond to skills taught in lesson

Automatic scoring: At the end of the SmartQuiz, the system automatically scores the results and shows you which skills you should review

Teaching Resources

The following is a list of supplemental material available with the Interactive Computing Series:

Skills Assessment

Irwin/McGraw-Hill offers two innovative systems, ATLAS and SimNet, which take testing beyond the basics with pre- and post-assessment capabilities.

ATLAS (Active Testing and Learning Assessment Software) – available for the Interactive Computing Series – is our live-in-the-application Skills Assessment tool. ATLAS allows students to perform tasks while working live within the Office applications environment. ATLAS is web-enabled and customizable to meet the needs of your course. ATLAS is available for Office 2000.

SimNet (Simulated Network Assessment Product) – available for the Interactive Computing Series – permits you to test the actual software skills students learn about the Microsoft Office applications in a simulated environment. SimNet is web-enabled and is available for Office 97 and Office 2000.

Instructor's Resource Kits

The Instructor's Resource Kit provides professors with all of the ancillary material needed to teach a course. Irwin/McGraw-Hill is dedicated to providing instructors with the most effective instruction resources available. Many of these resources are available at our Information Technology Supersite www.mhhe.com/it. Our Instructor's Kits are available on CD-ROM and contain the following:

Diploma by Brownstone - is the most flexible, powerful, and easy-to-use computerized testing system available in higher education. The diploma system allows professors to create an Exam as a printed version, as a LAN-based Online version, and as an Internet version. Diploma includes grade book features, which automate the entire testing process.

Instructor's Manual - Includes:
- Solutions to all lessons and end-of-unit material
- Teaching Tips
- Teaching Strategies
- Additional exercises

PowerPoint Slides - NEW to the Interactive Computing Series, all of the figures from the application textbooks are available in PowerPoint slides for presentation purposes.

Student Data Files - To use the Interactive Computing Series, students must have Student Data Files to complete practice and test sessions. The instructor and students using this text in classes are granted the right to post the student files on any network or stand-alone computer, or to distribute the files on individual diskettes. The student files may be downloaded from our IT Supersite at www.mhhe.com/it.

Series Web Site - Available at www.mhhe.com/cit/apps/laudon.

Digital Solutions

Pageout Lite - is designed if you're just beginning to explore Web site options. Pageout Lite is great for posting your own material online. You may choose one of three templates, type in your material, and Pageout Lite instantly converts it to HTML.

Pageout - is our Course Web site Development Center. Pageout offers a Syllabus page, Web site address, Online Learning Center Content, online exercises and quizzes, gradebook, discussion board, an area for students to build their own Web pages, and all the features of Pageout Lite. For more information please visit the Pageout Web site at www.mhla.net/pageout.

Teaching Resources (continued)

OLC/Series Web Sites - Online Learning Centers (OLCs)/Series Sites are accessible through our Supersite at www.mhhe.com/it. Our Online Learning Centers/Series Sites provide pedagogical features and supplements for our titles online. Students can point and click their way to key terms, learning objectives, chapter overviews, PowerPoint slides, exercises, and Web links.

The McGraw-Hill Learning Architecture (MHLA) - is a complete course delivery system. MHLA gives professors ownership in the way digital content is presented to the class through online quizzing, student collaboration, course administration, and content management. For a walk-through of MHLA visit the MHLA Web site at www.mhla.net.

Packaging Options - For more about our discount options, contact your local Irwin/McGraw-Hill Sales representative at 1-800-338-3987 or visit our Web site at www.mhhe.com/it.

Acknowledgments

The Interactive Computing Series is a cooperative effort of many individuals, each contributing to an overall team effort. The Interactive Computing team is composed of instructional designers, writers, multimedia designers, graphic artists, and programmers. Our goal is to provide you and your instructor with the most powerful and enjoyable learning environment using both traditional text and new interactive multimedia techniques. Interactive Computing is tested rigorously in both CD and text formats prior to publication.

Our special thanks to Trisha O'Shea, our Editor for computer applications and concepts, and to Jodi McPherson, Marketing Director for Computer Information Systems. Both Trisha and Jodi have provided exceptional market awareness and understanding, along with enthusiasm and support for the project. They have inspired us all to work closely together. Steven Schuetz provided valuable technical review of all our interactive versions, and Charles Pelto contributed superb quality assurance. Thanks to our new publisher, David Brake, and Mike Junior, Vice-President and Editor-in-Chief. They have given us tremendous encouragement and the needed support to tackle seemingly impossible projects.

The Azimuth team members who contributed to the textbooks and CD-ROM multimedia program are:

Ken Rosenblatt (Textbooks Project Manager and Writer)
Russell Polo (Chief Programmer)
Steven D. Pileggi (Interactive Project Manager)
Jason Eiseman (Technical Writer)
Michael Domis (Technical Writer)
Robin Pickering (Developmental Editor, Quality Assurance)
Raymond Wang (Multimedia Designer)
Michele Faranda (Textbook design and layout)
Stefon Westry (Multimedia Designer)
Caroline Kasterine (Multimedia Designer, Writer)
Tahir Khan (Multimedia Designer)
Joseph S. Gina (Multimedia Designer)
Irene A. Caruso (Multimedia Designer)
Josie Torlish (Quality Assurance)

Contents

FrontPage 2000 Brief Edition

Preface v

1 Introducing Microsoft FrontPage .... FP 1.1

Introducing Microsoft FrontPage .... FP 1.2
Starting FrontPage .... FP 1.4
Exploring the FrontPage Screen .... FP 1.6
Opening a Web Page .... FP 1.8
Saving a Web Page .... FP 1.10
Using Page View .... FP 1.12
Getting Help in FrontPage .... FP 1.14
Exiting FrontPage .... FP 1.16
Shortcuts .... FP 1.18
Quiz .... FP 1.19
Interactivity .... FP 1.21

2 Creating Web Sites .... FP 2.1

Creating a New Web Page .... FP 2.2
Creating a New Web Using a Template .... FP 2.4
Using a Web Wizard .... FP 2.6
Using the Import Web Wizard .... FP 2.10
Adding Text to a Web Page .... FP 2.12
Spell Checking and Editing a Web Page .... FP 2.14
Using the Find Command .... FP 2.16
Previewing a Web Page in a Browser .... FP 2.18
Shortcuts .... FP 2.20
Quiz .... FP 2.21
Interactivity .... FP 2.23

Contents

Continued

3 Formatting and Adding Objects to Web Pages...FP 3.1

Formatting Text on a Web Page......................................FP 3.2
Adding and Formatting Lists..FP 3.4
Creating Tables...FP 3.6
Formatting Tables...FP 3.8
Applying Themes to a Web...FP 3.10
Applying Custom Themes..FP 3.12
Creating Text Hyperlinks..FP 3.14
Editing Hyperlinks..FP 3.16
Adding Images...FP 3.18
Formatting Images...FP 3.20
Image Mapping..FP 3.22
Creating a Hover Button..FP 3.24
Creating a Marquee...FP 3.26
Inserting Text Boxes..FP 3.28
Adding Check Boxes and Radio Buttons........................FP 3.30
Creating a Drop-Down Menu..FP 3.32
Creating a Push Button...FP 3.34
Shortcuts..FP 3.36
Quiz..FP 3.37
Interactivity..FP 3.39

4 Publishing and Maintaining Web Pages...........FP 4.1

Creating a Web Hierarchy...FP 4.2
Adding a Navigation Bar...FP 4.4
Viewing and Printing the Web Structure.......................FP 4.6
Organizing Files in Folders View....................................FP 4.8
Verifying Hyperlinks..FP 4.10
Renaming Pages and Changing URL's...........................FP 4.12
Opening an Office Document in a Web.........................FP 4.14
Using the Office Clipboard..FP 4.16
Publishing a Web...FP 4.18
Shortcuts..FP 4.20
Quiz..FP 4.21
Interactivity..FP 4.23

Glossary..FP 1

Index..FP 11

- ▶ Introducing Microsoft FrontPage
- ▶ Starting FrontPage
- ▶ Exploring the FrontPage Screen
- ▶ Opening a Web Page
- ▶ Saving a Web Page
- ▶ Using Page View
- ▶ Getting Help in FrontPage
- ▶ Exiting FrontPage

INTRODUCING MICROSOFT FRONTPAGE

Microsoft FrontPage is a Web site authoring application. Web authoring programs are useful for quickly creating, editing, and enhancing Web pages, the basic units of Web sites. In general, you will find Web authoring programs are much faster in generating Web pages than raw HTML (hypertext markup language). A Web authoring program like Microsoft FrontPage provides an organized environment that will help you integrate graphics, text, and navigational elements. Just as important, you will learn how to create Web pages that are fun to use!

In this book you will learn how to use Microsoft FrontPage to create useful and attractive Web pages and Web sites. You are limited only by your imagination and your skill. You will learn how to add graphics and other effects to your Web pages to make them more effective. In addition, you will learn how to build e-commerce Web pages and sites that benefit businesses and other organizations.

Case Study:
Sydney Hanson is a professional Web site designer and a member of the Speed Demons, a national skydiving club. The Speed Demons are looking for someone to create a Web site for their club and she has offered her services. Primarily, they want their Web site to serve a dual purpose: to provide member services and to attract new members. They would also like it to be a resource for skydiving enthusiasts. Professional Web designers often design Web sites and train employees to maintain them.

Lesson 1 • Introducing Microsoft FrontPage

Introducing Microsoft FrontPage

Concept

While millions of people use the Web everyday, few know how Web pages and sites are actually built. Most Web users believe that building Web pages is quite complicated, and they are often intimidated by unfamiliar acronyms like HTML, HTTP, and URL.

In the past, authoring Web pages required knowledge of an editing language called HTML, hypertext markup language. While knowledge of HTML is still useful, there are new, more user-friendly Web authoring tools that make it possible for people to build Web pages without knowing HTML. The barriers to easy Web site construction are slowly but surely being erased. FrontPage 2000 enables you to design attractive and professional looking Web pages and sites with relative ease.

In the next four lessons you will learn the important basic steps in Web page and site design. First you will learn the basic elements of the FrontPage 2000 software: how to start the software, open a Web page, save a Web page, and get help. In the second lesson you learn how to create new Web pages, use the Web Wizard, and edit a Web page. In the third lesson you will learn how customize the Web page to achieve the objectives you want by adding hyperlinks, tables, and custom themes. In the fourth lesson you will learn how to organize, maintain, and publish Web pages.

Figure 1-1 provides an example of a Web Page in FrontPage 2000 and some of the features which may be added to a Web page.

Figure 1-1 Web Page in FrontPage 2000

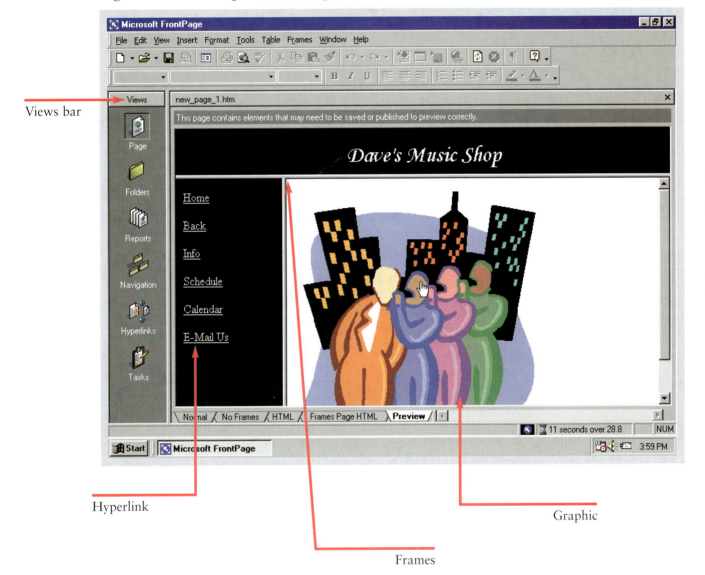

Lesson 1 • Introducing Microsoft FrontPage

Starting FrontPage

Concept

Before you can view or edit a Web page, you must open the FrontPage 2000 application. FrontPage opens with a new blank Web page file ready to format.

Do It!

In order to open the Web Page she wants to view, Sydney must start FrontPage.

1. Make sure the computer, monitor, and any other necessary peripheral devices are turned on. The Windows desktop should appear on your screen. Your screen may differ slightly from the one shown.

2. Locate the Windows taskbar, usually found at the bottom of your screen. Use your mouse to guide the pointer over the Start button [Start], on the left side of the Taskbar.

3. Click [Start] on the Windows taskbar. The Start menu appears.

4. Move the mouse pointer over the Programs folder to highlight it and open the sub-menu. The Programs submenu is displayed in **Figure 1-2**.

5. Position the pointer over Microsoft FrontPage icon to highlight it and click the left mouse button. FrontPage will open with a blank page, as shown in **Figure 1-3**.

More

Each computer varies in its set-up, depending on its hardware and software configurations. Therefore, your startup procedure may be slightly different from the one described above.

Notice that your mouse has two buttons to click. Whenever you are told to click a mouse button, click the left button, unless otherwise indicated.

FP 1.4

Figure 1-2 Windows Desktop

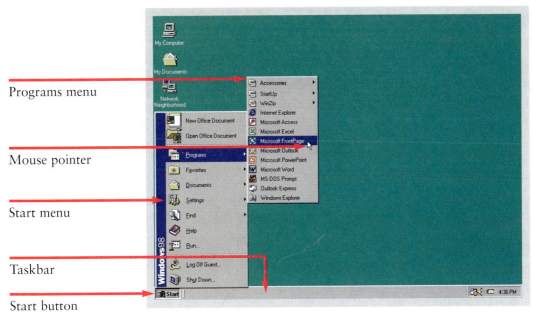

Programs menu

Mouse pointer

Start menu

Taskbar

Start button

Figure 1-3 FrontPage Window

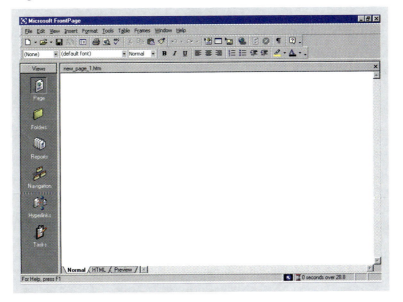

Lesson 1 • Introducing Microsoft FrontPage

Exploring the FrontPage Screen

Concept

FrontPage opens to a blank Web page enclosed in a frame. **View** buttons line the left side of the FrontPage window on the **Views bar**. The **Views bar** is a new feature of FrontPage 2000, which facilitates Web site management. The buttons on the Views bar are labeled according to the functions they control. These buttons are designed for working with **Webs**. A **Web** is a group of related interconnected **Web pages** intended to be explored as a **Web site**. A **Web page** is a document that can be viewed over the internet with its own **URL**, or **Uniform Resource Location**. A **Web site** is a group of Web pages that are linked together to form a cohesive, navigable Web. The FrontPage window is displayed in **Figure 1-4**.

The specific buttons on the Views bar are as follows:

Page: This button allows you to create and edit an individual Web page. Most formatting and the addition of graphics and other elements are done in this view.

Folders: This button enables you to view and organize the files and folders associated with a Web.

Reports: This view provides reports and updates on the status of files and hyperlinks, which enables you to keep your Web site up to date.

Navigation: This button displays the navigational structure of your Web site. You can also add navigation buttons to a Web page in this view.

Hyperlinks: This view displays every hyperlink to and from every page in a Web.

Tasks: This view lists the uncompleted tasks in a Web.

The remaining FrontPage window consists of the following elements:

Title bar: The bar running accross the top of the FrontPage window which contains the **Control menu** icon, the name of the application, and the **Sizing buttons** in the right-hand corner.

Sizing buttons: The **Minimize button** reduces the window to a program button on the Windows taskbar. The **Maximize button** will appear if the FrontPage window is not enlarged to fit the entire screen. The **Restore button**, which reverts the window to its previous size and location, will appear if the window is maximized. Finally, the **Close button** will close the application.

Menu bar: The row of menu titles below the Title bar. When you click a menu title, a drop-down list of commands related to the title appears.

Standard toolbar: The row of icons used to execute common commands.

Formatting toolbar: The row of list boxes and icons used to perform common text formatting commands.

Status bar: The bar on the bottom of the FrontPage window, that displays the activity being performed, active features, and the estimated downloading time.

Figure 1-4 FrontPage Window

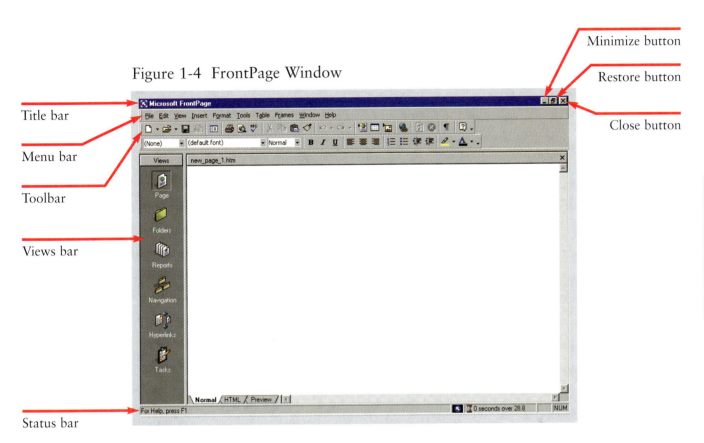

Lesson 1 • Introducing Microsoft FrontPage

Skill: Opening a Web Page

Concept

You will probably design your Web over a series of editing sessions. In order to work with a file you must know how to reopen it after you saved it. You must know the name of the file, and its location to open it.

Do It!

Sydney is going to open a Web page she created earlier.

1. Click **File**, on the Menu bar. The File menu opens.

2. Move the mouse pointer over **Open** to highlight it and click once. The **Open File** dialog box appears.

3. Click the drop-down arrow in the **Look in:** text box, as shown in **Figure 1-5**, to find the location of your **Student Files** folder. It may be located on a disk or in a folder on your desktop. If it is located on a disk you must highlight **3½ Floppy [A:]** to access it. If it is on your desktop, you must highlight the folder, and double-click to open any subsequent folders until you reach the desired file.

4. Once located, double-click the **Student Files** folder, and click on the **DoIt1-3** file.

5. Click .

6. The Web page **DoIt 1-3** opens, as shown in **Figure 1-6**.

More

Once you have created a Web, you can open its files by clicking the **Open Web** command on the **File** menu. The **Open Web** dialog box operates similarly to the **Open File** dialog box.

After you have created a Web or a file, you can bypass the **Open File** dialog box by clicking **File** on the Menu bar and highlighting **Recent Files**, or **Recent Webs**. The corresponding submenus will display the last Web pages or files you have accessed. These shortcuts are a new feature of FrontPage 2000.

If you open a file directly from its folder, it will open in your default **Web browser**. A **Web browser** is an application that enables you to view Web pages on the Internet. In order to edit a Web page however, you must open it from the FrontPage application.

Figure 1-5 Open File dialog box

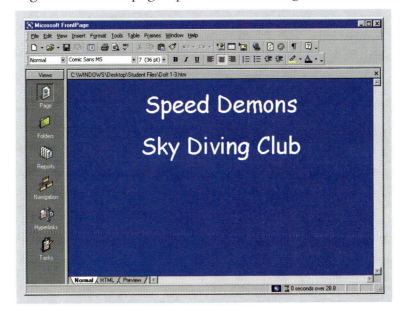

Location of floppy disk

Where future Webs may be kept

Click drop-down arrow to select location on desktop

Click to open file

Figure 1-6 Web page opened in FrontPage

Locate and open the file **Prac1-1** from your **Student Files** folder.

Folders can be located using the buttons on the left-hand side of the **Open File** dialog box instead of the down arrow button in the Look in: list box.

Lesson 1 • Introducing Microsoft FrontPage

Saving a Web Page

Concept

If you do not save your work, data can be lost due to power outages or computer failure. You can save Web pages to a hard drive, floppy disk, or network drive. If data is lost you can open your file to the most recently saved version therefore, it is important to frequently save your Web pages.

Do It!

Sydney will now save this Web page under a new name and in a new location.

1. Click **File** on the Menu bar.

2. Move the mouse pointer over **Save As** to highlight it.

3. Click once on **Save As**. The **Save As** dialog box opens.

4. The default folder is **myweb**, as shown in **Figure 1-7**. This folder is located in the **My Webs** folder, which is in the **My Documents** folder.

5. In the **File name:** text box type **skydive**, as shown in **Figure 1-8**.

6. Click [Save].

7. When you open the **myweb** folder again, the **skydive** Web page should be there with a logo next to it, also shown in **Figure 1-8**.

More

The **Save** command and the **Save As** command perform different functions. The first time you save a document, the **Save** command on the **File** menu, or the **Save** button on the Standard toolbar, will open the **Save As** dialog box. After you have named a file and stored it in a specific location, the **Save** command will simply overwrite the existing document. The **Save As** command will enable you to change the name and/or location of the document. It allows you to save and make changes to a document under a new name while maintaining the original file under the initial file name. Both commands are accessed from the **File** menu.

Webs are saved in folders entitled myweb. The more pages and Webs you create the more myweb folders there are. The next Web you create will be saved as myweb1, then myweb2, and so on.

Figure 1-7 Save As dialog box

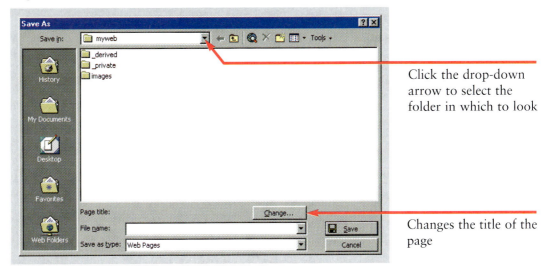

Click the drop-down arrow to select the folder in which to look

Changes the title of the page

Figure 1-8 Web Page saved in folder

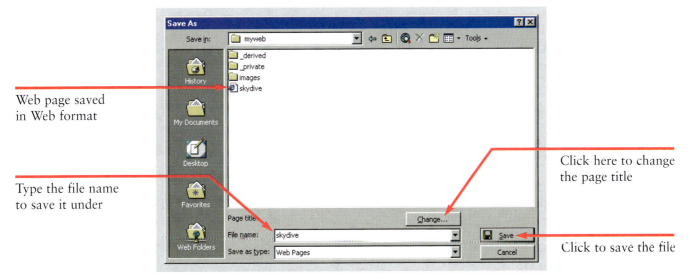

Web page saved in Web format

Type the file name to save it under

Click here to change the page title

Click to save the file

Save the file **Prac 1-1** as **Caddy** in the **myweb** folder.

You can create a customized folder in any location by clicking the **Create New Folder** button in the **Save As** dialog box.

Lesson 1 • Introducing Microsoft FrontPage

Using Page View

Concept

Most Web page designing is done in **Page** view. Text, graphics and other Web elements are added and reformatted in Page view. There are three formats available for viewing Web pages: **Normal**, **HTML**, and **Preview**.

Do It!

Sydney is going to view her Web page in the three formats provided by **Page** view.

1. Open the **skydive** Web page in **FrontPage**.

2. Click the **Page** button on the **View** bar if it is not already selected.

3. Three tabs are located on the lower left-hand side of the window. Click the **HTML** tab. This view displays your page in **HTML** format, as shown in **Figure 1-9**.

4. Click the **Preview** tab. The page will be displayed in a browser window. You cannot format or edit your page from the Preview tab. You can only use this format to click on hyperlinks, and preview your visual effects. The **Preview** format is displayed in **Figure 1-10**. Since no effects have been added however, it looks the same as Normal format.

More

FrontPage is an **HTML editor**. It takes the work you create and edit in **Normal** view and converts it into **Hypertext Markup Language** or **HTML**. If you know **HTML**, you can create a page using the **HTML** tab rather than the **Normal** tab. The results of your work can always be viewed in the **Preview** tab.

Figure 1-9 Web page in HTML format

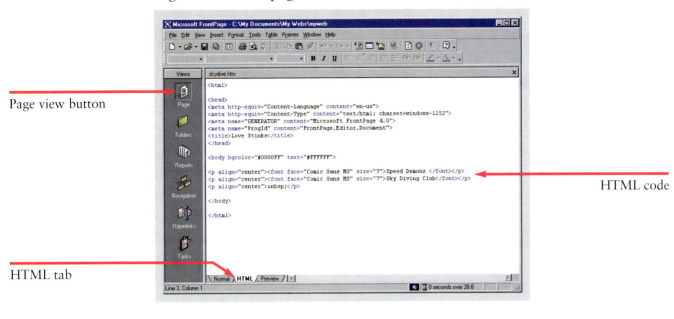

Page view button

HTML code

HTML tab

Figure 1-10 Web page in Preview format

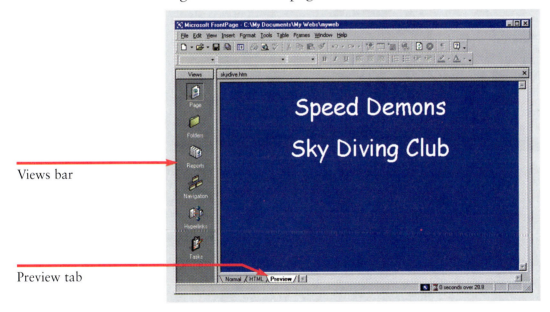

Views bar

Preview tab

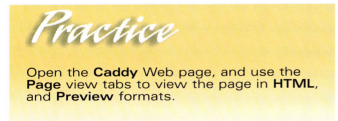

Open the **Caddy** Web page, and use the **Page** view tabs to view the page in **HTML**, and **Preview** formats.

Page view is the only view explicitly used for creating, editing, and enhancing your Web pages. The other views are primarily used for managing your Web.

Lesson 1 • Introducing Microsoft FrontPage

Getting Help in FrontPage

Concept

FrontPage has several help options. The FrontPage Help window has three tabs: Index, Contents, and Answer Wizard.

Do It!

Sydney will use the Help window tabs to find out about three different views.

1. Click Help on the Menu bar.

2. Click the Microsoft FrontPage Help command, the Microsoft FrontPage Help dialog box opens on the right side of the screen.

3. Click the Index tab.

4. In the Type keywords text box type Reports. You will automatically receive a list of Help topics, as shown in **Figure 1-11**.

5. Double-click on Reports_view in the Or choose keywords box. Read what it says about Reports view.

6. Click the Answer Wizard tab. In the What would you like to do text box, type in What is Navigation view.

7. Click Search.

8. The Select topic to display: window provides an index of related topics, as shown in **Figure 1-12**.

More

All three Help tabs direct you to the same information. If you are unsure of exactly what you are looking for, the Contents tab allows you to search an expandable table of contents. General topics are listed next to book icons. Clicking the plus sign to the left of the book icon will access a list of more specific subtopics. The Index tab uses keywords to locate topics. It is useful if you know the name of the feature you wish to explore. The Answer Wizard enables you to request help topics by asking a question in your own words.

The Hide button, in the upper left-hand corner of the FrontPage Help window, reduces the window to one section. The Hide button is then replaced by the Show button, which in turn, expands the Help window back to the two-paneled format.

Another Help feature is the What's This? command. It is also accessed from the Help menu. When you click the Whats This? command the pointer turns into a. When you click a particular button, or other screen element with this pointer, a screen tip appears describing its function in further detail.

Figure 1-11 Index help feature

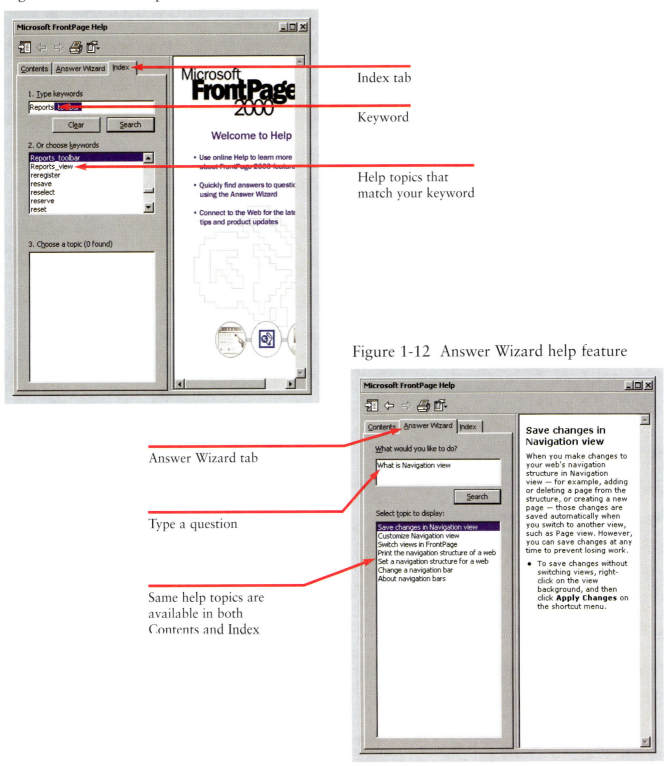

Figure 1-12 Answer Wizard help feature

Practice

Using whatever feature you feel most comfortable with, look up information on **Folders**, **Hyperlinks**, **Tasks**, and **Page** views.

Hot Tip

At the top left of the Help window are navigation buttons. You can use these buttons to move back and forth between topics you have already viewed.

Lesson 1 • Introducing Microsoft FrontPage

Exiting FrontPage

Concept

It is important to properly exit the FrontPage application. Exiting and closing the application properly will prevent data loss.

Do It!

Sydney has finished using FrontPage for the day, and is going to exit the program.

1. Open the skydive Web page.

2. Click File on the Menu bar.

3. Move the pointer over Exit to highlight it.

4. Click Exit once, as shown in Figure 1-13.

5. If you have made changes to the page without saving them the Warning dialog box shown in Figure 1-14 appears. Clicking [Yes] saves the changes and closes FrontPage. Clicking [No] closes the program without saving the changes, and clicking [Cancel] stops the program from closing.

6. If you have not made any changes, FrontPage simply closes.

More

There are other ways to close a file and exit Front Page. The easiest method is to use the Close buttons [X]. The Close button on the Title bar closes the application, while the Close button in the upper right-hand corner of the Front Page window closes the active Web page.

There is no keyboard shortcut for exiting FrontPage, however, there is one for closing the active file. Instead of using the File menu, you can press [Control] and F4 on the keyboard simultaneously to close the active Web page.

Figure 1-13 Exiting FrontPage

- File menu
- Closes page without exiting application
- Closes page and exits application
- Close button
- Close file button

Figure 1-14 Warning dialog box

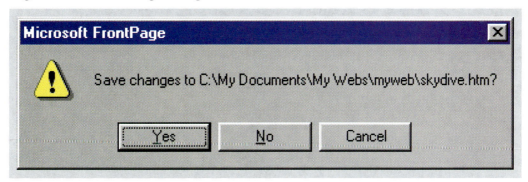

Open the **Caddy** Web page. Then close the file and exit FrontPage.

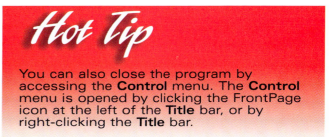

You can also close the program by accessing the **Control** menu. The **Control** menu is opened by clicking the FrontPage icon at the left of the **Title** bar, or by right-clicking the **Title** bar.

Shortcuts

Function	Button/Mouse	Menu	Keyboard
Open File		Click File, then click Open	[Ctrl]+[O]
Open Web		Click File, then click Open Web	
Save File		Click File, then click Save	[Ctrl]+[S]
Microsoft FrontPage Help		Click Help, then click Microsoft FrontPage Help	F1
What's This?		Click Help, then click What's This?	[Shift]+F1
Page view		Click View, then click Page	

Identify Key Features

Name the items indicated by callouts in **Figure 1-15**.

Figure 1-15 Components of the FrontPage window

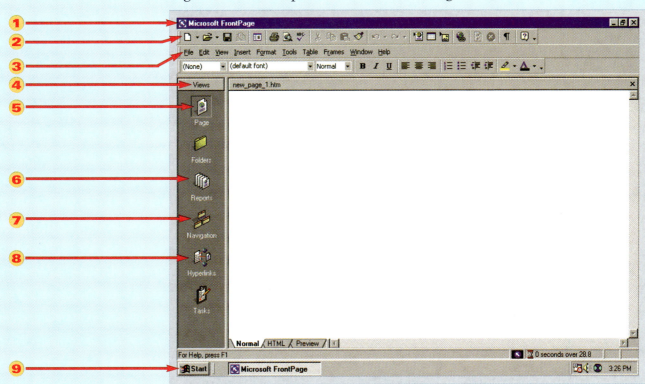

Select The Best Answer

10. Creating, editing and most Web page formatting is done here
11. The Web page address
12. This help feature looks up keywords
13. Overwrites an existing document
14. An assortment of Web pages that make up a Web site
15. The Start button is found here
16. Displays activities being performed and active elements at the bottom of the screen
17. Buttons at the top right of the window that allow you to alter the size of the window

a. Save
b. Windows taskbar
c. Page View
d. Sizing buttons
e. Index
f. Status bar
g. Web
h. URL

Quiz (continued)

Complete the Statement

18. The Contents tab is part of this feature:
    a. Views bar
    b. Menu bar
    c. The Help Window
    d. Status

19. Click this command to open a recently worked on Web site:
    a. File
    b. Recent Web
    c. Open File
    d. Old Web

20. This view gives you updates on your files and hyperlinks so that you can keep your Web up to date:
    a. Reports view
    b. Page view
    c. Hyperlinks view
    d. Update view

21. If you open a Web page directly from an icon in one of your desktop folders:
    a. It will not open at all
    b. All data will be lost
    c. It will open in FrontPage to will be able to edit it
    d. It will open in your browser to will be unable to edit it

22. This Help feature enables you to click items to access screen tips.
    a. Index
    b. Contents
    c. Answer Wizard
    d. What's this?

23. This contains graphical buttons that execute specific commands:
    a. Standard toolbar
    b. Menu bar
    c. Graphical toolbar
    d. Taskbar

24. The Control menu is accessed from the:
    a. File menu
    b. Taskbar
    c. Title bar
    d. Menu bar

25. The formatting language used to create Web pages:
    a. URL
    b. Web code
    c. FrontPage 2000 code
    d. HTML

Interactivity

Test Your Skills

1. Opening FrontPage 2000:

    a. Start FrontPage by using the Start menu, accessed from the Windows taskbar.

    b. Click the different view buttons on the Views bar.

2. Open a Web Page:

    a. Click **File**, then click **Open**.

    b. Locate your **Student Files** folder.

    c. Locate the Web Page **Test 1**, and open it.

3. Save a Web Page:

    a. Click **File**, then click **Save As**.

    b. Locate the **mywebs** folder, in the **My Documents** folder.

    c. Save the file as **watertaxi**.

4. View a Web Page in Page View:

    a. Open the **watertaxi** page.

    b. Click the **Page View** button on the **Views** bar, if it is not already selected.

    c. Click the **HTML** tab.

    d. Click the **Preview** tab.

5. Getting help in FrontPage:

    a. Click **Help**, then click **Microsoft FrontPage Help**.

    b. On the **Contents** tab, find the section on **Pages** under the heading, **Designing Web Pages**.

    c. On the **Index** tab type in the key word **Graphic** and see what comes up.

6. Exiting FrontPage:

    a. Click **File**, then click **Exit**.

    b. Do not save any changes that you made since you last saved **watertaxi**.

Interactivity (continued)

Problem Solving

Congratulations. You have been hired by Diggs & Associates as an Office Assistant. Your position is primarily involved with the creation and maintenance of a Web site for a small publishing house, Diggs & Associates. In order to maintain a competitive advantage, they realized they would need a Web site to distribute information to agents, authors, and other potential business partners. Furthermore, they realized that certain business transactions could be conducted via the Internet.

Your first job is to devise a rough draft of a Web site. Nothing concrete is necessary, just a few conceptual proposals including thematic examples and possible features. Some possible features to consider are a product ordering page and a guest book to record visitors to the site.

Make a list of the Web site components you advocate. Use your imagination, be creative and brainstorm. All of your ideas may not be plausible but many can come to fruition. For example, images complete with animation can be added. Plug-ins and applets are other possibilities. These terms will be explained in future lessons if you are unfamiliar with them.

Devise a personally significant Web site. For example, if you are a soccer enthusiast, create a soccer Web site. Consider what type of information will be relevant and useful to visitors and what sites might complement yours. Search the Internet for related sites to link to yours.

Find one or more Web sites that you like and compile a list of the attributes that attracted you to them. Take detailed notes about what makes these sites attractive and engaging to visitors. Your notes should include everything from animation and graphics to theme, color, writing style, font size, and font color.

- ▶ Creating a New Web Page
- ▶ Creating a New Web Using a Template
- ▶ Using a Web Wizard
- ▶ Using the Import Web Wizard
- ▶ Adding Text to a Web Page
- ▶ Spell Checking and Editing a Web Page
- ▶ Using the Find Command
- ▶ Previewing a Web Page in a Browser

LESSON 2

CREATING WEB SITES

After you have planned a Web site, the next step is to create the necessary Web pages. This can be accomplished in several different ways.

You can start from scratch with the blank page that automatically appears when you open the FrontPage application, or use a wizard or a template to create a new page. In this lesson we will show you how to use wizards and templates. A Wizard is a series of dialog boxes that guides you through the creation process. A template is a preformatted Web page containing sample text and pictures that a Web author copies and edits to create their own unique page.

Wizards and templates can also be used to create entire Webs. The Wizard will build a rough Web, complete with a Home page, and the general organization and style of your choice.

In addition this lesson will teach you the fundamental tasks of adding, editing and spell checking text. You will learn how to find and replace specific words or subjects and how to preview a published Web page.

Case Study:
Sydney will begin planning her Web site. The planning process will include a period of trial and error in which she creates various Web pages and Webs using several different methods. This process will prepare her to design a functional and appealing Web site for the Speed Demons.

Lesson 2 • Creating Web Sites

Creating a New Web Page

Concept

The fundamental building block of a Web site is one or several Web pages. One of the easiest ways to get started building Web pages is to use templates that are predefined by FrontPage. Templates can be easily modified to suit your specific needs.

Do It!

Sydney is going to create a new Web page.

1. Click **File**, on the **Menu** bar.

2. Highlight **New**, and click **Page** from the submenu that appears.

3. The **New Page** dialog box opens.

4. Click the **Guest Book** page, as shown in **Figure 2-1**.

5. Click [OK].

6. The new Web page appears in the FrontPage window complete with **placeholder text**, as shown in **Figure 2-2**. **Placeholder text** displays the text format and facilitates data entry.

More

A **template** is a basic structure or outline. FrontPage has many useful templates from which to choose. Some templates are specifically designed to accommodate graphics, some come equipped with radio buttons, still others have predesigned return forms. Take advantage of these templates to create functional Web pages.

Directly below and to the right of the FrontPage window are **scroll bars** equipped with **scroll boxes** and **scroll arrows**. Clicking the right or left **scroll arrow** on the horizontal **scroll bar** will move the view to the right or left. Clicking the up or down **scroll arrow** on the vertical **scroll bar**, will move the screen up or down one line at a time.

You can move more quickly by clicking and dragging the **scroll boxes** up, down, left or right. The size of the **scroll box** changes with the page size. The longer a page is top to bottom, the shorter the vertical **scroll box**. As page width increases, horizontal **scroll box** size decreases.

Figure 2-1 New Page dialog box

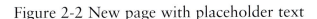

Web page templates and wizards

Description of the type of page you are creating

Allows you to preview what the template looks like

Figure 2-2 New page with placeholder text

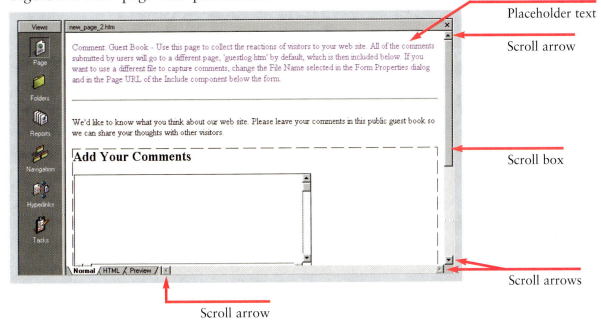

Placeholder text

Scroll arrow

Scroll box

Scroll arrows

Scroll arrow

Practice

Open FrontPage and create a new Web page using whatever template you want.

Hot Tip

Cascading style sheets, available in the **New Page** dialog box, offer a wider range of style options than standard HTML.

Lesson 2 • Creating Web Sites

Creating a New Web Using a Template

Concept

A new Web can be started as easily as a new Web page. If you have an idea of the theme and format you want, you can create one using a template. A Web template will create an entire Web site with a Home page and a general organizational structure and outline. You will overwrite placeholder text with your own data.

Do It!

Sydney is going to create a Web using a preconstructed template.

1. Click File on the Menu bar.

2. Highlight New, and click Web from the submenu that appears.

3. The New Web dialog box appears. Select the Customer Support Web, as shown in Figure 2-3.

4. Click [OK].

5. Your Web is created, complete with a Home page.

6. To view the structure of the Web, click the Navigation button on the Views bar.

7. This site is displayed in Figure 2-4.

More

Every Web contains a Home Page. A Home page is the first page a visitor sees when they reach a site. Links are used to navigate between the various pages in the Web.

The New Web dialog box provides a description of each available template. The Customer Support Web furnishes a feedback mechanism to improve customer support services. The Project Web provides a team member directory and enables project team members to discuss ideas and concerns, post status reports, and schedule meetings. A Personal Web consists of a Home page, a Photo album page, an Interests page, and a page which links to the author's favorite sites.

Each of these Web templates serves different purposes, however, a template is not a restrictive structure. Web templates can be edited and reorganized. Themes can be applied during or after the creation process. Unnecessary pages can be deleted and additional pages can be inserted. For example, if a company wants to advertise using multiple photographs, the Web author can begin with the Personal Web template and add a Form page and a Guest book page. Start with a Web template that is suited to your requirements and edit it in any way you wish to make it your own.

FP 2.4

Figure 2-3 New Web dialog box

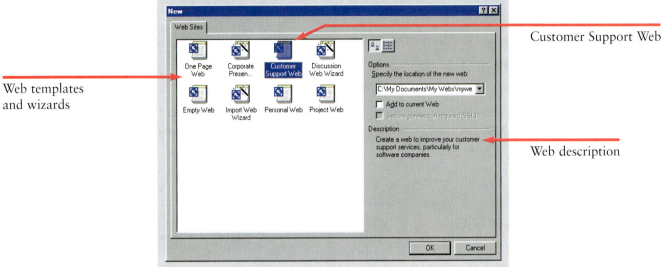

Web templates and wizards

Customer Support Web

Web description

Figure 2-4 New Web with placeholder text

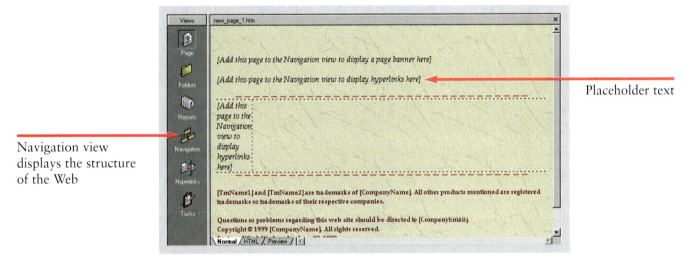

Placeholder text

Navigation view displays the structure of the Web

Practice

Create a **Project Web** to be used with the **Caddy** page.

Hot Tip

Most Web servers require a default name for Home pages, usually, **Index.htm**. If you change it, FrontPage will automatically rename it if required by the server, when you publish the Web.

Lesson 2 • Creating Web Sites

Using a Web Wizard

Concept

A wizard is an automated procedure that conveniently performs a complex operation. A series of dialog boxes prompts you to choose options that accomplish the task to your specifications. The quickest easiest method for creating a Web is to choose a Web Wizard.

Do It!

Sydney is going to use a wizard to create a new Web.

1. Click **File**, on the Menu bar.

2. Highlight **New**, and click **Web** from the submenu that appears.

3. The **New Web** dialog box appears. Click the second icon from the left, the **Corporate Presence Wizard**, and click [OK].

4. The first dialog box is an introduction to the Wizard, shown below in **Figure 2-5**. Click [Next >].

5. The next dialog box allows you to choose the pages to include in your Web. Make sure that all of the check boxes are checked, except for the **Products and Services** box. Click [Next >].

6. The next dialog box is a description of the Home page. Only check the **Mission Statement** and **Contact Information** boxes, as shown in **Figure 2-6**. Click [Next >].

7. The next dialog box describes the **What's New** page. Click the **Articles and Reviews**, and **Web Changes** check boxes, as shown in **Figure 2-7**. Click [Next >].

8. The next dialog box sets up the **Feedback Form**. Leave the default settings selected and click the **Mailing Address** check box, as shown in **Figure 2-8**. Click [Next >].

Figure 2-5 Corporate Presence Web Wizard dialog box

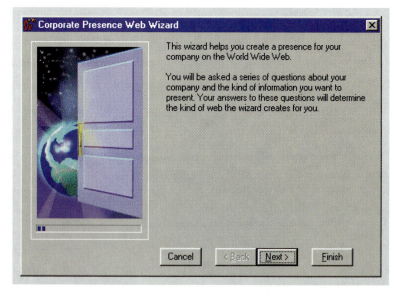

FP 2.6

Figure 2-6 Web Wizard dialog box

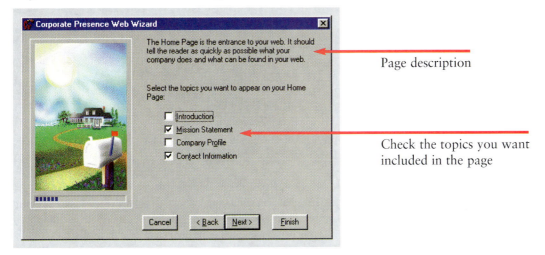

Page description

Check the topics you want included in the page

Figure 2-7 Web Wizard dialog box

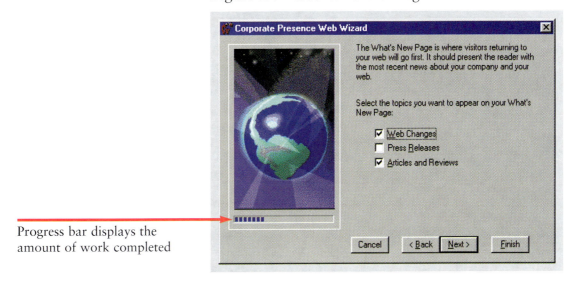

Progress bar displays the amount of work completed

Figure 2-8 Web Wizard dialog box

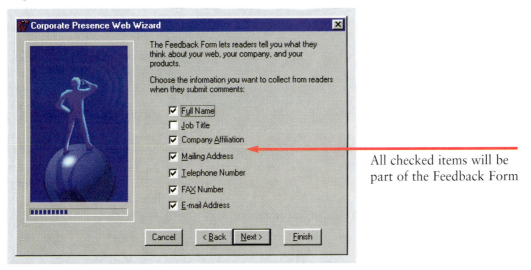

All checked items will be part of the Feedback Form

Lesson 2 • Creating Web Sites

Using a Web Wizard (continued)

Do It!

9 Accept the default settings, and click Next>.

10 The next dialog box sets up the Table of Contents. Click the Keep page list up-to-date automatically check box, and click Next>.

11 The next dialog box adds objects to the top and bottom of each page. Leave the default settings checked. In addition click the check boxes to place the company logo at the top of each page, and click the Date page was last modified at the bottom of each page, the dialog box is shown in Figure 2-9. Click Next>.

12 Accept the default setting, and click Next>.

13 Click in the company name text box to place the insertion point there. Delete the sample company name and type Speed Demons Sky Diving Club. Type in Skydiver as the one word version of that name. The address is 345 Rocky Rd., Falling Water, N.Y. 10566, as shown in Figure 2-10. Click Next>.

14 The telephone number and the fax number are the same, (914) 728-9903. The Webmaster's e-mail address is Shanson@domain.skydiver.com. The e-mail address for general info is info@domain.speed_demon.com. Click Next>.

15 Click Next>, without choosing a Web theme.

16 Click Finish. The Web opens in Tasks view, the only tasks are for you to customize the pages. Click the Navigation view button, see Figure 2-11.

More

Web Wizards are most useful when creating a complicated Web, they will guide a user through the process of creating a complicated site. You can use wizards to create a Form Page, which is used to collect information from the user. You can also create Data Access Pages, which are Web pages created using Microsoft Access databases. You can create a Personal Web, which includes a photo album you can use for picture. There is also a Discussion Web Wizard, a Customer Support Web Wizard, and an Import Web Wizard.

You can type in the specified location of your Web folder in the Specify the Location of the New Web text box in the New Web dialog box. FrontPage will create a new folder with a specified name. For example, type C:\Windows\Desktop\Sydney's Web\, FrontPage will create a folder on your desktop called Sydney's Web. If you do not place the Windows before Desktop then the folder will be created in your Desktop folder on the hard drive.

The first letter specifies the drive where the folders are located. Generally A: is the floppy disk drive, C: is the hard drive, and D: is the CD Rom drive. Then specify the location, such as Desktop, or My Documents, this method can help you save a Web anywhere on your computer.

Figure 2-9 Web Wizard dialog box

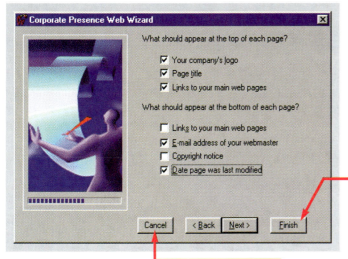

You can finish the wizard at any time

You can cancel the wizard at any time

Figure 2-10 Web Wizard dialog box

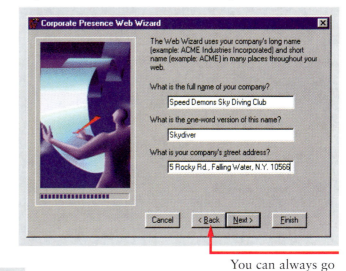

You can always go to the previous step in the wizard

Figure 2-11 Web in Navigation view

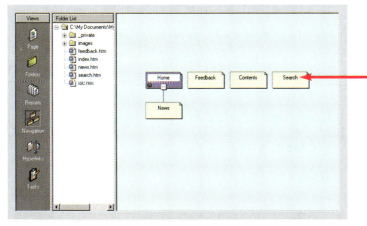

Go to a page by clicking on it in Navigation view

Practice

Create a **Corporate Presence Web** for the **Caddy** file. The Company name and address appear in the file. Only provide the information already contained in the file.

Hot Tip

If you do not specify the name of the folder or the location in which to save it, FrontPage will create a default folder called **myweb**. Each succeeding Web will be labeled **myweb1**, **myweb2**, **myweb3**, etc.

Lesson 2 • Creating Web Sites

Using the Import Web Wizard

Concept

When you import a file to FrontPage you are essentially creating a new Web using preexisting files. A wizard has been created to make the importing process easier. The Import Web Wizard creates a new Web, while also importing data from another file.

Do It!

Sydney will use the Import Web Wizard to create a new Web, by importing data from an preexisting files.

1. Click File on the Menu bar.

2. Highlight New, and click Web from the submenu that appears. The New Web dialog box opens. Click on the Import Web Wizard. In the Specify the Location of the New Web text box type C:\My Documents\Skydiver\. As shown in Figure 2-12. This means that the Web will be saved in a folder called Skydiver in the My Documents folder. Click [OK]. The first Import Web Wizard dialog box opens.

3. Click the From a source directory of files on a local computer or network radio button. Click the [Browse...].

4. In the Browse for Folder dialog box locate your Student Files folder, and click Doit2-5 as shown in Figure 2-13. Click [OK]. Click the Include subfolders checkbox and click [Next >].

5. Click [Next >] again, then click [Finish].

6. Double-click the Index file in the Skydiver Web. It is the original Skydiver page you worked with earlier.

More

FrontPage opens your Web to a blank page. To open a previously saved Web page, double-click the page icon beneath the folder it is located in, in the Folder List. You can also click the Navigation button on the Views bar and double-click the page you want to view on the Navigation structure. At present, in Navigation view, the Skydiver Web contains only one page. Double-clicking it will open the Speed Demons page in Page view.

FP 2.10

Figure 2-12 New Web dialog box

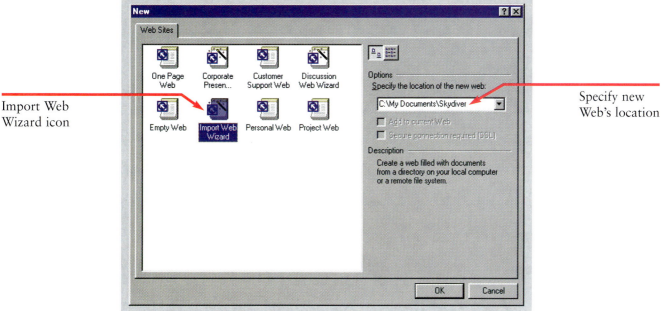

Import Web Wizard icon

Specify new Web's location

Figure 2-13 Browse for Folder dialog box

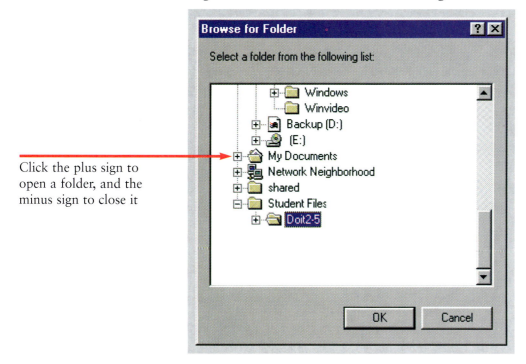

Click the plus sign to open a folder, and the minus sign to close it

Practice

Import **Prac2-8** into a new Web you create called **Caddy Shop**. Place the new folder wherever you would like.

Hot Tip

You can use the **Import Web Wizard** to transfer data from a published Web site to a new Web as well as to convert a folder to a Web.

FP 2.11

Lesson 2 • Creating Web Sites

Adding Text to a Web Page

Concept

Perhaps the most important job in creating a Web site is composing the text. Imparting information to visitors to your site is after all, your primary goal. Adding text is the first step in the creation of a functional Web site.

Do It!

Sydney has created her Web, and will begin adding text to the imported Home page.

1. Open the Speed Demons page in Page view from the Skydiver Web.

2. Move the pointer over the text. The pointer turns into an I-beam. If the color of the background is colored, than the I-beam color may change.

3. Move the I-beam to the end of the word Club, and click. A flashing insertion point, a black bar which marks where text will be added, should appear at the end of Club. The insertion point also changes with the background color, as shown in Figure 2-14.

4. Press the [Enter] key on your keyboard four times.

5. Type: A National Organization for those who live on the edge. Your page should look like Figure 2-15.

6. Click File, then click Save.

7. Close the Index page.

More

In Lesson 3, you will learn how to format or change the appearance of text, using the Formatting toolbar. Text formatting includes font, font style, size, color and alignment. Special effects can even be added to enhance the way text appears.

FP 2.12

Figure 2-14 Insertion point placed in text

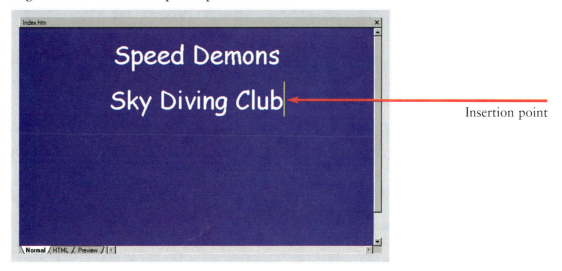

Insertion point

Figure 2-15 Page with new text added

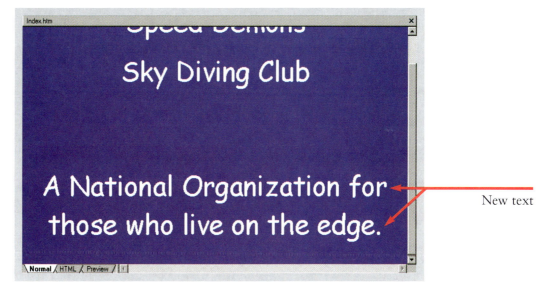

New text

Practice

Five lines below the last line of text on the **Index** page in the **Caddy Shop** Web, type: **Best Prices this Side of the Pond.**

Hot Tip

The **[Tab]** key on the keyboard moves text several spaces, generally toward the right, depending on the format you apply. You can use the **[Enter]**, **[Tab]** key, and **[Space bar]** to effect where on a page text appears.

Lesson 2 • Creating Web Sites

Spell Checking and Editing a Web Page

Concept

Typing errors are inevitable. While adding text to a Web page in the Normal tab, you can use the Spell Checker to locate mistakes. Underlines will alert you to possible errors. Editing text is then a fairly simple task.

Do It!

Sydney is going to check one of her Web pages for spelling errors, and make the neccessary corrections.

1 Open the page Doit2-6 from your Student Files folder.

2 Click Tools on the Menu bar, then click Spelling.

3 The Spelling dialog box automatically opens when it reaches a word that is not in its dictionary, as shown in **Figure 2-16**.

4 Click [Change].

5 Click [Cancel].

6 Place the I-beam I behind the k in the misspelled word, and click to place the insertion point. The misspelled word is shown in **Figure 2-17**.

7 Press the [Backspace] key on the keyboard to delete the k.

8 Type rm, so the word determine is spelled correctly.

9 Save the file as Writing Tips in your My Documents folder.

More

Clicking [Add] will add a word to the spell checking dictionary. This is particularly useful if the checker frequently stops on your name, or for unusual words that are not in the dictionary. You can also highlight and right-click a word to access a shortcut popup menu. The shortcut menu will contain a list of possible replacements and the Add and Ignore commands.

FP 2.14

Figure 2-16 Spelling dialog box

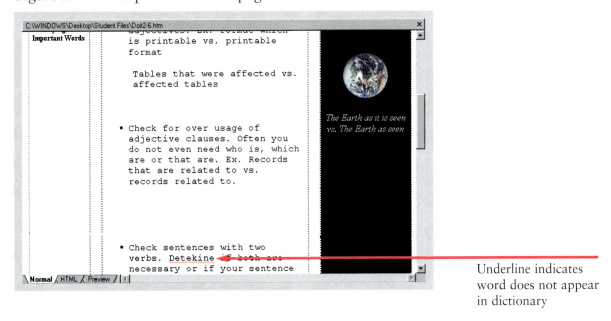

List of possible replacements for misspelled word

Ignores word not in dictionary

Ignores all words of same spelling

Changes all errors to suggested word

Changes error to suggested word

Figure 2-17 Misspelled word in page

Underline indicates word does not appear in dictionary

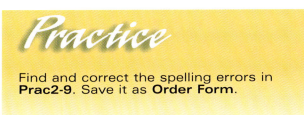

Find and correct the spelling errors in **Prac2-9**. Save it as **Order Form**.

When a word is underlined in red, it indicates that it is not in the dictionary. You can do on-the-spot editing without accessing the **Spell Checker**.

Lesson 2 • Creating Web Sites

Using the Find Command

Concept

Quickly locating specific words or phrases can be difficult in a lengthy page or Web. The FrontPage Find and Replace commands enable you to search for and review or edit text quickly and accurately.

Do It!

Sydney is having difficulty with her adverb clauses. She will find the section on adverb clauses on her Writing Tips page.

1. Open the Writing Tips page.

2. Click Edit on the Menu bar, then click Find.

3. The Find dialog box opens, as shown in Figure 2-18.

4. In the Find what: text box type adverb clauses.

5. Click [Find Next]. The Find command takes you to the first mention of adverb clauses.

6. Click [Find Next] again. The Find command takes you to the second occurrence of adverb clauses, as shown in Figure 2-19.

7. Click [Cancel].

8. Close the page.

More

The Replace command is also accessed from the Edit menu. The Replace dialog box is almost identical to the Find dialog box. However, an additional text box enables you to enter replacement text. Two additional buttons enable you to replace a single instance, [Replace] or all instances of a particular word or phrase, [Replace All]. In the Search section options section, radio buttons allow you to choose to search the entire document or just the current page. In the Direction section you can choose to search up or down the document.

The Replace command may be on the extended Edit menu. Not all commands are on the primary menu. In Office 2000, menus automatically expand after a few seconds. You can hasten the process by moving the pointer over the double arrows at the bottom of the menu. Primary menu commands will include commands you have recently used.

Figure 2-18 Find dialog box

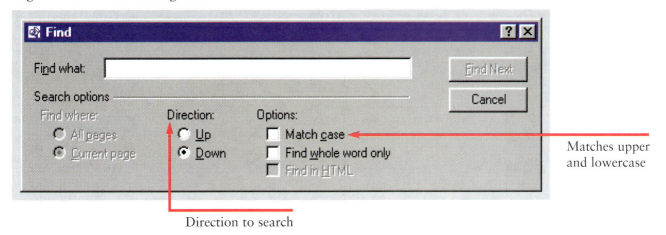

Matches upper and lowercase

Direction to search

Figure 2-19 Text found in page

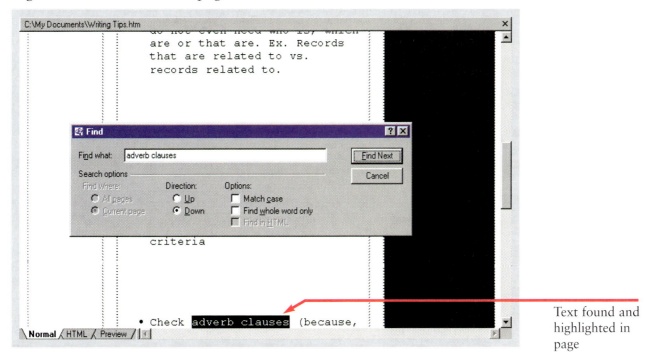

Text found and highlighted in page

Practice

Open the **Order Form** and find a question that asks the user to enter their **age**.

Hot Tip

You can use the **Find** and **Replace** commands in almost every different view. You can also use them to find and replace text in **HTML**.

Lesson 2 • Creating Web Sites

Previewing a Web Page in a Broswer

Concept

FrontPage Webs will look exactly as you see them in Internet Explorer 4 or above, but may look very different in other browsers. Even simple Web pages will display differently depending on the browser used. The Preview tab in Page view, displays a Web as it will appear online. However, the Preview in Browser command will give you an even better idea of how your Web pages will look when published. A browser, as you will recall, is a program that enables you to view Web pages and HTML documents.

Do It!

Sydney is going to preview her Web in her browser to see how it looks.

1. Open the Skydiver Web.

2. Open the Index page.

3. Click File on the Menu bar. Then click the Preview in Browser command. It may appear on the extended menu.

4. The Preview in Browser dialog box opens, as shown in Figure 2-20.

5. Click Preview.

6. The browser opens with your page displayed, as shown in Figure 2-21.

7. Close the browser.

8. Close FrontPage.

More

If you click on a file directly from the folder it's in, rather than opening it in FrontPage, then it will open in your default browser without going through the process of the Preview in Browser dialog box.

FP 2.18

Figure 2-20 Preview in Browser dialog box

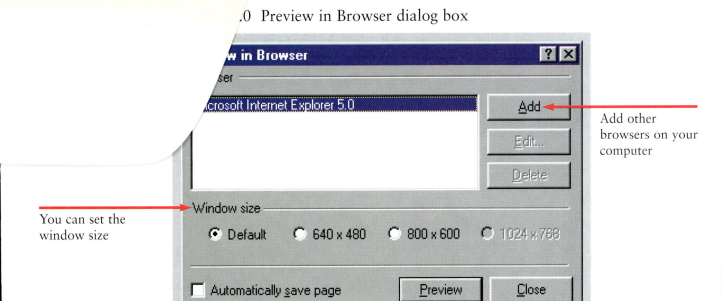

Add other browsers on your computer

You can set the window size

Figure 2-21 Web page previewed in browser

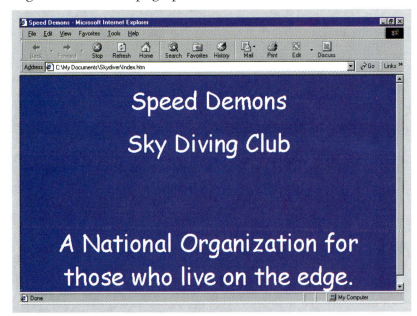

Open the **Caddy Shop** file, and preview it in your browser.

As long as they are in good working order, your hyperlinks will operate when you preview a page in your browser. You can link to other pages in a Web or to Web sites on the Internet.

Lesson 2 • Creating Web Sites

Shortcuts

Function	Button/Mouse	Menu	Keyboard
New Page		Click File, then click New, then click Page	[Ctrl]+N
New Web		Click File, then click New, then click Web	
Preview in Browser		Click File, then click Preview in Browser	
Find		Click Edit, then click Find	[Ctrl]+F
Replace		Click Edit, then click Replace	[Ctrl]+H
Check Spelling		Click Tools, then click Spelling	F7

INTERACTIVE COMPUTING • FrontPage 2000

Identify Key Features

Name the items indicated by callouts in **Figure 2-22**.

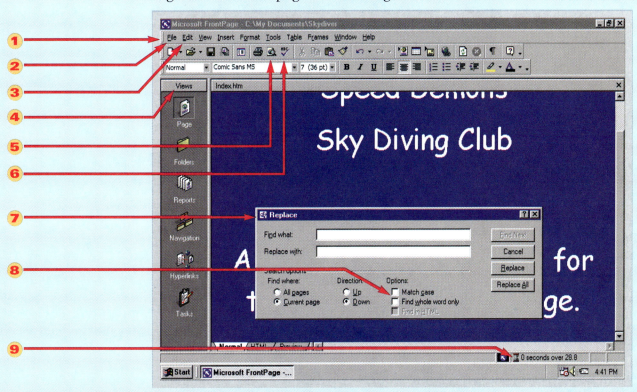

Figure 2-22 Web page in FrontPage

Select The Best Answer

10. A series of dialog boxes that facilitates the creation of a Web page or an entire Web
11. A preconstructed document that allows you to fill in your own content
12. Allows you to type text directly onto the page
13. The pointer turns into this when it is held over the FrontPage screen
14. This feature allows you to search by the case of the first letter in a word
15. A word will be flagged by the Spell Checker if it does not appear here
16. The first Web page you visit in a Web site
17. Allows you to view Web pages and HTML documents

a. Match case
b. I-beam
c. Template
d. Browser
e. Dictionary
f. Wizard
g. Insertion point
h. Home page

Lesson 2 • Creating Web Sites

(continued)

...he Statement

... New Web commands can be ...

19. A Web page that is created using a database from Microsoft Access is called a:
    a. Form page
    b. Data Access page
    c. Home page
    d. Discussion page

20. If you open a file directly from a folder, rather than opening it in FrontPage:
    a. It will open in FrontPage anyway
    b. It will open in a Web editor
    c. It will open in a Browser
    d. It will not open at all

21. Some commands cannot be found on the regular menu, sometimes you must open:
    a. An extended menu
    b. A folder
    c. A wizard
    d. A keyboard shortcut

22. When you use either the Find or Replace command, you have the option of searching a page:
    a. Left-to-right, right-to-left
    b. By the size of the word
    c. Up or down
    d. By the verb tense

23. When creating a Web using the Import Web Wizard you must select the folder to import using:
    a. The Find Folder command
    b. The Browse for Folder dialog box
    c. The Find Folder dialog box
    d. The Edit menu

24. If you misspelled a word while typing, FrontPage alerts you:
    a. By highlighting the word
    b. By automatically changing the word
    c. By underlining the word in red
    d. By having a dialog box open automatically

25. The computer hard drive is usually marked by the letter:
    a. D
    b. E
    c. A
    d. C

Interactivity

Test Your Skills

1. Create a new Web page using a template:
   a. Click **File**, then **New**. Click **Page** from the submenu that appears.
   b. Select a template from the ones provided in the **New Page** dialog box.

2. Create a new Web with a template:
   a. Click **File**, then click **New**. Click **Web** from the submenu that appears.
   b. Select the **Personal Web Wizard** from the **New Web** dialog box.
   c. Save the Web as **My Site**.

3. Create a Web using a Web Wizard:
   a. Click **File**, then **New**. Click **Web** from the submenu that appears.
   b. Select **Corporate Presence Wizard** from the **New Web** dialog box.
   c. Create a **Corporate Presence Web** using the options provided.

4. Import a Web:
   a. Click **File**, then **New**. Click **Web** from the submenu that appears.
   b. Select the **Import Web Wizard**.
   c. Create a Web called **Water Taxi**.
   d. Import the **Test 2** Web from your **Student Files** folder to the **Water Taxi** Web.

5. Add and Edit Text:
   a. Fix the spelling error that occurs in the **Test 2** file.
   b. Below the table, type in a slogan for the Water Taxi service.
   c. Place the insertion point at the end of the table. Press the **[Enter]** key until you are four lines below the table.
   d. Add the slogan.

6. Preview a Web page in a browser:
   a. Make sure **Test 2** is open.
   b. Click **File**, then click **Preview in Browser**.
   c. Select a Browser.
   d. Close the browser, and FrontPage, and save as **Water Taxi**.

Interactivity (continued)

Problem Solving

Use the **Corporate Presence Wizard** to create a Web site for Diggs & Associates. Name the Web folder **Diggs** and save it in your **My Documents** folder. Keep your earlier plans in mind. You can always add pages to a Web to accommodate your various ideas. Include a **Products/Services** page. Accept the default settings for the **Products/Services** page. Fill in the name of the company, **Diggs & Associates**, the address, **987 Park Lane**, **Tompson MA 02411**, and the telephone number, **(582) 690-9043**. The fax number is **(582) 690-1649**. Your e-mail address is the Webmaster's address. The general info address is: **info@domain.diggs.com**. Leave the default settings for everything else.

Your supervisors think you should add a product-ordering page. They have asked you to design a prototype for their perusal. Use the **Form Page Wizard**, found in the **New Page** dialog box, to give them an idea of what a product-ordering page will look like. In the first dialog box, click **Add** to affix ordering information to the page. Leave the default settings for everything else.

Another Diggs employee is interested in previewing the Web site. He has asked you to create a blank Web using the **Corporate Presence Wizard**, to give him a rough idea of the site structure. Change the options in various ways to create several versions to show him.

Create your personal Web site. Use a template or a wizard if appropriate. You can start with a blank page and write a short bio, if you like. Create an entire Web or merely a Home page. Experiment and let your creativity flow.

- ▶ **Formatting Text on a Web Page**
- ▶ **Adding and Formatting Lists**
- ▶ **Creating Tables**
- ▶ **Formatting Tables**
- ▶ **Applying Themes to a Web**
- ▶ **Applying Custom Themes**
- ▶ **Creating Text Hyperlinks**
- ▶ **Editing Hyperlinks**
- ▶ **Adding Images**
- ▶ **Formatting Images**
- ▶ **Image Mapping**
- ▶ **Creating a Hover Button**
- ▶ **Creating a Marquee**
- ▶ **Inserting Text Boxes**
- ▶ **Adding Check Boxes and Radio Buttons**
- ▶ **Creating a Drop-Down Menu**
- ▶ **Creating a Push Button**

LESSON 3

FORMATTING AND ADDING OBJECTS TO WEB PAGES

Formatting to make your site aesthetically pleasing is a difficult task. It is crucial, however, in order to attract visitors to your site. If you use a template, with preformatted text, you may not bother with formatting. However, as you become more adept at creating your own Web pages, you will probably want to exert more control over the final product.

Tastes are extremely variable and subjective. The Microsoft FrontPage program offers many possibilities for designing Webs to suit various styles and sensibilities.

Applying a theme is perhaps the easiest formatting method. The font or typeface, text color, background, bullet style, and graphics are chosen all at once. This saves time, and complementary elements have been chosen for you.

Adding objects takes practice and experience. Certain objects are more effective in specific situations. Lists, tables, hyperlinks, and images can be added to your pages and formatted to your specifications.

Forms can be added to Web pages or created as independent pages. Text boxes, radio buttons, check boxes, and drop-down menus can be added to forms to gather information from Web site visitors. After answering questions, with the help of these various form fields, the visitor clicks a Submit button to send the data to the server.

After you add objects to a Web page you must know how to reformat them, move them, change their colors, size, and borders, and even add animation. Learning these skills will enable you to produce an appealing, high quality Web site.

Case Study:
Sydney has designed a basic structure for her Web. Now, she will add objects for organizational and aesthetic purposes. She will reformat text, add a theme, and experiment with other formatting options to enhance the Speed Demons Web.

Lesson 3 • Formatting and Adding Objects to Web Pages

Formatting Text on a Web Page

Concept

FrontPage allows for many formatting options. These formatting options include changing the font or typeface, font style, font size, color and alignment. Text can be aligned to the left, right, or center. It can be underlined, italicized, or made bold. Many formatting commands can be accessed from the Formatting toolbar, which is directly above the FrontPage window.

Do It!

Sydney is going to change the font, and decrease the font size of the secondary text.

1. Open the **Skydiver** Web, to the **Index** page.

2. Click and hold the **I-beam** I in front of the letter **A**, in the second phrase. Click and drag the pointer to the end of the phrase, highlighting it. The text should appear as shown in **Figure 3-1**.

3. Click the drop-down arrow in the **Font Size** list box on the **Formatting toolbar**, the toolbar is shown in **Figure 3-2**.

4. Select the size **5 (18 pt)** from the drop-down list. The highlighted paragraph becomes smaller.

5. Click the drop-down **Font** list box, seen in **Figure 3-2**.

6. Scroll down until you get to the font **Monotype Corsiva** font. Click it to select it. The text is changed to the new font.

7. Highlight the first two lines of the page.

8. Click the **Underline** button U on the Formatting toolbar.

9. Click once anywhere on the screen to deselect the highlighted text.

10. Your page should now resemble **Figure 3-3**.

11. Save the file.

More

The word **Font** refers to typeface style. Some fonts are bold, some are ornate, some are classic. You can choose a comical or a serious font to set the tone for your page.

Next to the Underline button are the **Bold** B and **Italic** I buttons, which can be used together or separately. The three style buttons are especially useful for headers, footers and other text you want to stand out.

The three layout buttons, align left, align right, and center control where text appears on the page. Sometimes you must use the alignment buttons in conjunction with the space bar to arrange text exactly as desired.

INTERACTIVE COMPUTING • FrontPage 2000

Figure 3-1 Page text highlighted

Highlighted text

Figure 3-2 Formatting toolbar

Style list box Font list box Drop-down arrows Font size box Bullets button Numbering button Decrease and increase indents buttons Font color button Highlight button

Figure 3-3 Formatted text

Underline style applied

New size and font

Practice

On the Index page of the **Caddy Shop** Web, format the text so that the address of the shop appears in the font **Century Gothic**, and is underlined.

Hot Tip

If you apply a format before typing, it will be applied to the entire page. If you highlight the target text, on the other hand, the formatting will be applied only to the selected section.

Lesson 3 • Formatting and Adding Objects to Web Pages

Adding and Formatting Lists

Concept

FrontPage has many ways of organizing information on a Web Page. One simple and convenient way for organizing information on a Web page is to create a list. Lists consolidate information in a concise format. They can either be numbered or bulleted using the corresponding buttons on the Formatting toolbar.

Do It!

Sydney is going to add a new page to her Skydiver Web.

1. Open the Skydiver Web.

2. Open the Index page.

3. Click File on the Menu bar and highlight New. Click Page from the submenu that appears. Click Normal Page, then click OK. A new page opens.

4. Type: Organizational Goals. Then click the Center button. Select the text and format it so that the font is Arial Black and the size is 5 (18pt).

5. Click and place the insertion point after s in Goals. Press the [Enter] key.

6. Click the Align Left button. Then click the Bullets button. Type: Increase club membership. Press the [Enter] key again. Type: Increase public awareness.

7. Follow the same procedure to create a list that includes: Catch media attention, Stress safety measures, and Make skydiving more affordable and enjoyable for all. The page is shown in Figure 3-4.

8. Right-click one of the bullets in the list. Click List Properties. The List Properties dialog box opens.

9. Click the bullets that are empty circles, as shown in Figure 3-5, and click OK.

10. Save the file in the Skydiver Web, accept the default name, organizational_goals.html.

More

You can create a numbered list rather than a bulleted list using the Numbering button. Then, you can right-click an item in a numbered list to access the shortcut popup menu. In the Numbers tab of the List Properties dialog box you can choose to label your list with capital or lowercase letters or Roman numerals.

Figure 3-4 Bulleted list

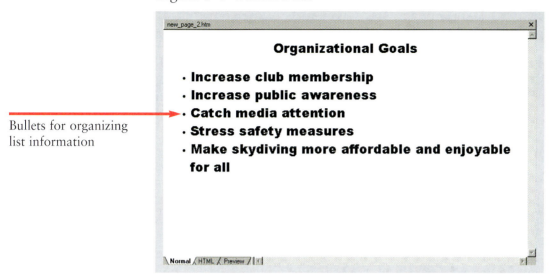

Bullets for organizing list information

Figure 3-5 List Properties dialog box

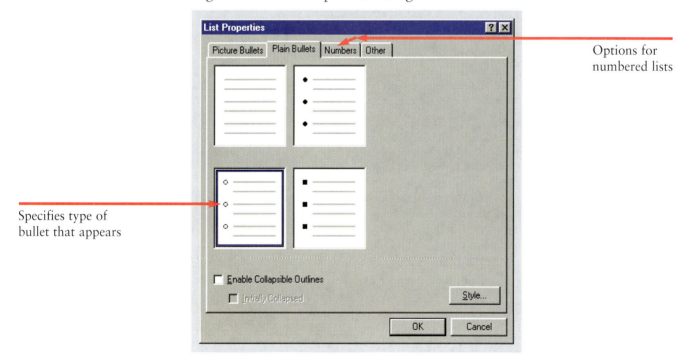

Options for numbered lists

Specifies type of bullet that appears

Practice

Create a new page in the **Caddy Shop** Web. At the top write **Best selling items**. Then create a numbered list, listing, in order, **Tees**, **Balls**, **Clubs**, **Bags**, **Shoes**, **Shirts**, **Pants**, **Videos**, **Books**.

Hot Tip

To change the properties of only one item in the list, right-click the item you want to change and select **List Item Properties** from the shortcut menu. The List Item Properties dialog box will open presenting formatting options for that particular item.

Lesson 3 • Formatting and Adding Objects to Web Pages

Creating Tables

Concept

Tables are commonly used on Web pages to organize information in a structured and attractive way. To start, all you need is a rough outline and a general idea of where you want to insert the table. Tables consist of cells containing blocks of text or numbers. Tables can be imported from Microsoft Word or Microsoft Excel, so that you can reuse existing tables from word processing or spreadsheet documents.

Do It!

Sydney is going to insert a table into her Index page in the Skydiver Web.

1. Open the Index page from the Skydiver Web.

2. Place the insertion point halfway between the slogan for the club, and the underlined name of the club.

3. Click Table on the Menu bar. Then highlight Insert, and click Table from the submenu.

4. The Insert Table dialog box opens, as shown in Figure 3-6.

5. Click OK to accept the default settings.

6. The table is created with the insertion point in the first cell.

7. Type: Organizational Goals. Press the [Tab] key.

8. Type: Schedule of Events, Recent News, and Skydiving Near You, pressting the [Tab] key after each entry.

9. When you have finished entering the text, save the file. Your page should now look like Figure 3-7.

More

The Insert Table button on the Standard toolbar can also be used to create a table. A box appears in which you move the pointer to highlight the desired number of cells. If you want to change any of the cell properties, however, you should use the Table menu and go through the Insert Table dialog box.

The number and size of the rows and columns does not have to be decided ahead of time. As you add content to your table, the rows and columns will expand. To add two more entries to the table you just created, simply press the [Tab] key at the end of the text in the fourth cell. Another row with two cells will automatically be inserted.

Figure 3-6 Insert Table dialog box

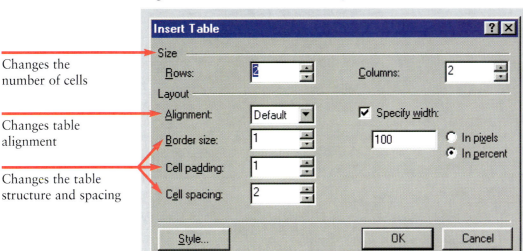

Changes the number of cells

Changes table alignment

Changes the table structure and spacing

Figure 3-7 Page with table inserted

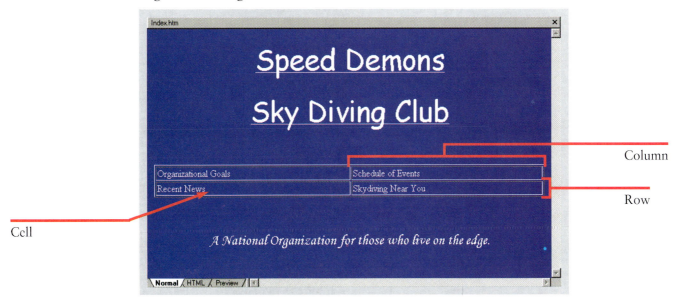

Column

Row

Cell

Practice

Insert a table into the **Index** page of the **Caddy Shop** Web. Add the following text; **Sales**, **Products**, **Contact us**, and **Employment**, into the four cells.

Hot Tip

You can create a table without borders by changing the **Border size**, **Cell padding**, and **Cell spacing** to **0** in the **Insert Table** dialog box.

Lesson 3 • Formatting and Adding Objects to Web Pages

Formatting Tables

Concept

Formatting can be applied to tables after they are created. Text formatting including font changes, underlining and color can also be added. The Table Properties dialog box will enable you to add background colors, apply various borders, and adjust the spacing between cell contents and cell walls. Changes can be made to the entire table, individual cells or specific rows or columns. You can also use the pointer to resize the table.

Do It!

Now that it is inserted into the page, Sydney will format the table she created.

1. Right-click the border of the table.

2. Click Table Properties from the shortcut menu. The Table Properties dialog box opens.

3. Click the drop-down list in the Color list box in the Borders section. Click on the white color square. Click Apply.

4. Change the Light Border and Dark Border to white. Click Apply.

5. Change the Background Color to the same blue background as the page. Click Apply. The Table Properties box should look like Figure 3-8.

6. Click OK. Right-click the border. Click Cell Properties from the shortcut menu. The Cell Properties dialog box opens.

7. Click the drop-down arrow on the Horizontal Alignment list box in the Layout section. Click Center from the drop-down list.

8. Click Apply and then OK. Notice that only one cell is affected. Click and drag to select the entire table and right-click. Reopen the Cell Properties dialog box and repeat the procedure to center the remaining cells. When you have finished your page should look like Figure 3-9.

More

You can use the pointer to resize a table, move the pointer over the border you want to move. If you want to resize the table horizontally, move the pointer over a vertical border, and the pointer will turn into a horizontal resizing arrow ↔. If you want to resize the table vertically, move the pointer over a horizontal border and it will turn into a vertical resizing arrow ↕.

Once the pointer has turned into a resizing arrow, simply click and drag the border until it is the size that you want.

To add rows or columns, click and drag to select the table. Click Tables on the Menu bar. Click Insert, then click Rows or Columns. Use the Insert Rows or Columns dialog box to insert the rows or columns you want.

FP 3.8

Figure 3-8 Table Properties dialog box

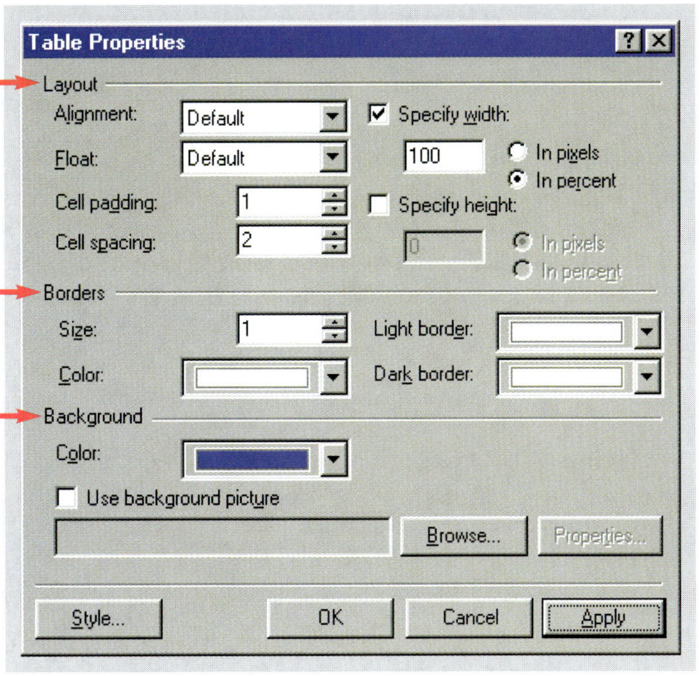

Layout section

Borders section

Background section

Figure 3-9 Formatted table on a page

Border colors are changed, and text is centered within cells

Practice

Format the table on the Index page in the **Caddy Shop** Web so that the borders are all the same color green as the text.

Hot Tip

If you click **Font** on the shortcut menu, the **Font** dialog box will open, allowing you to change the font, color, and other aspects of the text.

Lesson 3 • Formatting and Adding Objects to Web Pages

Applying Themes to a Web

Concept

A theme is a preformatted style that can be applied to a Web page or an entire Web. A set of formatting instructions controls the background, fonts, colors, and button styles. Themes provide a fast method for designing Webs or applying a matching design to multiple pages.

Do It!

Sydney will apply a theme to her Skydiver Web.

1. Open the Index page from the Skydiver Web.

2. Click Format on the Menu bar.

3. Click Theme. The Themes dialog box opens.

4. In the selection box on the left, click on Blends to highlight it. A preview appears, as shown in Figure 3-10.

5. Make sure that the All Pages radio button is selected. Click [OK].

6. A warning message appears telling you that you will be permanently replacing formatting information. Click [Yes].

7. It takes FrontPage several seconds to apply the theme. When it does your page should resemble Figure 3-11.

8. If you open the organizational_goals page, you will notice the formatting has been applied to that page as well.

9. Save these changes.

More

You can also use the Themes dialog box to apply a theme to only one page in a Web. In Navigation view, double-click on the target page to open it. Open the Themes dialog box, select the theme, and click the Selected page radio button, which appears beneath the All pages radio button. The theme will only be applied to the selected page. To remove a theme click No Theme in the Themes dialog box. Applying themes is a new feature that has been added to FrontPage 2000.

Figure 3-10 Themes dialog box

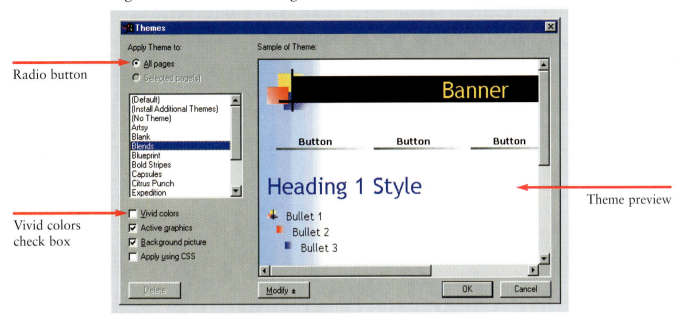

Radio button

Vivid colors check box

Theme preview

Figure 3-11 Web with theme apllied

Theme is applied to all FrontPage elements

Practice

Apply the **Citrus Punch** theme to the **Caddy Shop** Web.

Hot Tip

Clicking the **Vivid colors** check box in the **Themes** dialog box will bring out brightly colored text and graphics in the themes.

Lesson 3 • Formatting and Adding Objects to Web Pages

Applying Custom Themes

Concept

One of the reasons themes are so useful, is because they do not restrict the user to the prechosen format. Even though colors, fonts, etc., have already been selected, FrontPage allows you to make changes to these features. Knowing how to make these changes will allow you to work with existing themes, to create a customized theme.

Do It!

Now that Sydney has selected a theme for her Web, she is going to make changes and customize that theme.

1. Open the Index page of the Skydiver Web.

2. Click Format, click Theme. The Themes dialog box opens. Click the All Pages radio button.

3. Click the Vivid colors check box.

4. Click the Expedition theme to highlight it.

5. Click [Modify]. Several new buttons appear below the preview window.

6. Click [Colors]. The Modify Theme dialog box opens, as shown in Figure 3-12.

7. Click [Text...]. The Modify Themes dialog box reopens. Body should be selected in the Item: list box. Click the Comic Sans MS font to highlight it. As shown in Figure 3-13. Click [OK].

8. Click [Save As..] in the Themes dialog box. The Save Theme dialog box opens. Type New Theme as the title of the theme.

9. Click [OK]. Close the Themes dialog box.

10. Save the changes. Your custom theme should look like Figure 3-14.

More

The Color Wheel tab in the Modify Theme dialog box can be used to select customized colors for your theme. The color intensity can also be adjusted on the Brightness bar. Your selections can be previewed on the right-hand side of the dialog box, allowing you to precisely fine-tune your color scheme.

FP 3.12

Figure 3-12 Modify Theme dialog box

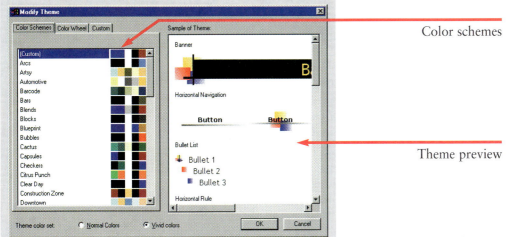

Figure 3-13 Text modification

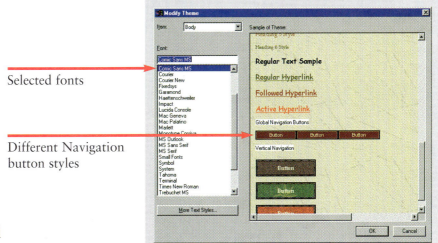

Figure 3-14 New theme applied

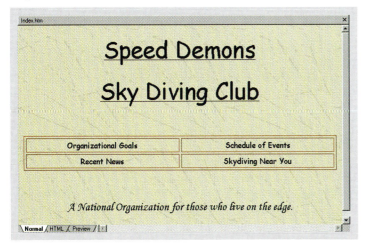

Practice

Add a customized theme to the **Caddy Shop** Web. Apply the **Capsules** theme and modify it using the **Cactus** color scheme. Change the body text to **Garamond**.

Hot Tip

You can use the **Graphics** button to add background images to your Web. Click  and locate the desired image to incorporate it into the Web background.

Lesson 3 • Formatting and Adding Objects to Web Pages

Creating Text Hyperlinks

Concept

A hyperlink is an object in a Web page that connects a visitor to a file, another Web page or another Web site. Hyperlinks can be designed to download files or start other operations. They can also link to e-mail addresses. Almost any object, word, or image can be used to create a hyperlink.

Do It!

Sydney is going to create hyperlinks in her Skydiver Web to link the pages in the Web.

1. Open the Index page in the Skydiver Web.

2. Highlight Organizational Goals in the table.

3. Click Insert on the Menu bar, then click Hyperlink. The Create Hyperlink dialog box opens.

4. In the dialog box window click the organizational_goals page, as shown in Figure 3-15.

5. Click [OK]. The hyperlink is created. The text changes color, and is underlined.

6. Highlight Recent News in the table. Click Insert, then Hyperlink.

7. Double-click in the URL: box, and type: recent_news.htm. Click [OK].

8. Follow the same procedure to create hyperlinks to the target URL's schedule_of_events.htm, and skydiving_near_you.htm.

9. Save the changes. Click the Preview tab.

10. Notice that when you move the pointer over a hyperlink it turns into a 👆, as it would in a browser. Click the Organizational Goals hyperlink. The Organizational Goals page is displayed.

11. Your page should now look like Figure 3-16.

More

There are four buttons to the right of the URL list box. The first, 🌐, enables you to use your Web browser to link to a selected page or file. The second button, 📁, enables you to link to a file on your computer. The third button, ✉, enables you to create a link that sends e-mail. When the user clicks the link, their default mail program opens to a mail-composing window with the specified e-mail address inserted. The final button, 📄, creates a new page, then automatically links to that new page.

You can create a hyperlink without choosing a specific word, phrase or image on the Web page. Simply place the insertion point where you want to position the hyperlink. Access the Create Hyperlink dialog box and locate the target page or file. When you create the link, the title of the target page will be inserted on the Web page. If there is no title, the URL will be inserted.

Figure 3-15 Create Hyperlink dialog box

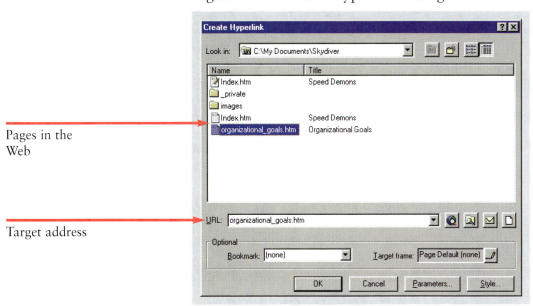

Pages in the Web

Target address

Figure 3-16 Hyperlinks on a page

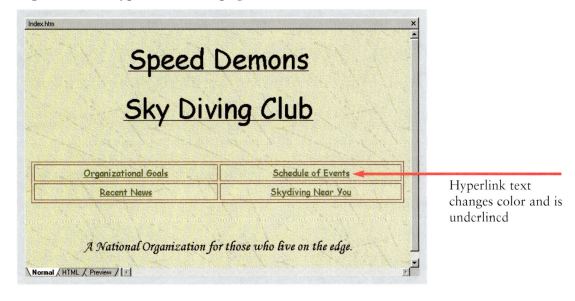

Hyperlink text changes color and is underlined

Practice

Create four hyperlinks for the four items in the table on the **Index** page in the **Caddy Shop** Web. The addresses are **sales.htm**, **best_selling_items.htm** (for **Products**), **employment.htm**, and the e-mail address **luckycaddy@domain.caddy.com**.

Hot Tip

When you move the pointer over a link in **Page** view, the target address is displayed in the Status bar. Check the hyperlink by holding the **[Ctrl]** key and clicking the link.

Lesson 3 • Formatting and Adding Objects to Web Pages

Editing Hyperlinks

Concept

It is often necessary to edit hyperlinks. Page names or target addresses may change. You may want to switch from one kind of link to another, for example, change a URL link to an e-mail address link. Microsoft FrontPage 2000 makes it easy to change links after they are inserted.

Do It!

Sydney has decided to make some changes to the hyperlinks she created earlier.

1. Open the Index page of the Skydiver Web.

2. Right-click the Schedule of Events hyperlink.

3. Click Hyperlink Properties from the shortcut menu. The Edit Hyperlink dialog box opens, as shown in **Figure 3-17**.

4. Click . Click Normal Page in the New Page dialog box, click OK .

5. Click File from the Menu bar, and select the Save As command to save the new page under the name calendar. Change the title to Calendar by clicking the Change button to the right of the default Page title, New Page 1. Be sure to save it in the Skydiver Web.

6. Double-click the Index page to open it. Move the pointer over the Schedule of Events hyperlink. Hold [Ctrl] and click the hyperlink. The link takes you to the new calendar page.

7. Reopen the Index page and right-click the Skydiving Near You hyperlink. Follow the same procedure to name the new page local and change the title to Local. Repeat the procedure for the Recent News hyperlink. Click File and choose the Save As command to name the page news and change the title to News.

More

Changes can be made to hyperlink text the same way you make changes to regular text. You can use the Formatting toolbar to change the font, font color, font size, and font style of hyperlink text. If hyperlinks are in different locations on the page however, you will probably have to change each hyperlink individually. With the hyperlinks in the table structure, you can simply select it and reformat the table.

If there is no theme applied you can change the format of hyperlinks on a page by right-clicking, then click Page Propeties from the shortcut menu, then click the Background tab. The Background tab of the Page Properties dialog box is displayed in **Figure 3-18**.

To change the text color of all the hyperlinks in a Web at once, access the Custom tab in the Color section of the Modify Theme dialog box. In the Item: list box, select Hyperlinks and choose a color from the Color: list box.

The easiest way to create a hyperlink is to type the URL of the target page directly onto the Web page. FrontPage will automatically create a link to the specified Web address.

Figure 3-17 Edit Hyperlink dialog box

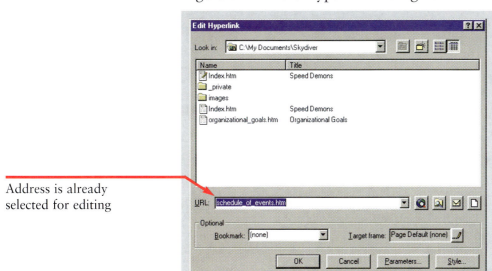

Address is already selected for editing

Figure 3-18 Page Properties dialog box

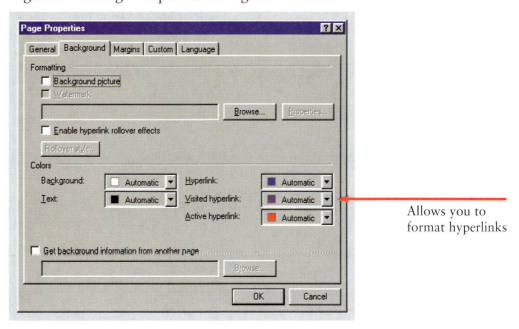

Allows you to format hyperlinks

Practice

Create new pages to link to and from the **Caddy Shop Index** page. Title the new pages **Sales** and **Employment**. Be sure to save them in the **Caddy Shop** Web.

Hot Tip

To delete a hyperlink, access the **Edit Hyperlink** dialog box and delete the text in the **URL** list box. The text or image that you used to activate the link will remain on your Web page. You can also delete the hyperlink text directly from the Web page.

Lesson 3 • Formatting and Adding Objects to Web Pages

Adding Images

Concept

Images can add informative content to a Web page or simply augment its style. You should keep in mind, however, that each picture lengthens a page-loading time. The Microsoft Clip Art Gallery allows you to quickly add graphics and photos to your Web page.

Do It!

Sydney will insert an image from the Microsoft Clip Art Gallery into the Index page in her Skydiver Web.

1. Open the Index page from the Skydiver Web.

2. Place the insertion point between the title of the club and the table.

3. Click Insert on the Menu bar. Click Picture, then click Clip Art from the submenu that appears. The Microsoft Clip Art Gallery opens.

4. Click in the Search for clips: text box to highlight the text and press the [delete] key. Type: air, and press the [Enter] key. The results of the search are shown in Figure 3-19.

5. Click the clip on the left. A small menu of buttons appears, as shown in Figure 3-20.

6. Click the top button, Insert Clip.

7. The image is inserted as shown in Figure 3-21.

8. Save the file. The Save Embedded Files dialog box will open. Click [OK]. This will save the image in the Skydiver Web. If the image is not saved with the Web, or is accidentally saved in a folder in another Web, it will not appear with the published Web.

More

Images are sometimes so large that they prevent a Web page from loading in a reasonable amount of time. Be sure to check the loading time on the Status bar.

The best formats to save images in are GIF (Graphic Interchange Format), and JPEG (Joint Photographic Experts Group). These formats compress large photographic files so that they do not take as long to load when published. Images you insert that are not in GIF or JPEG format will be automatically converted to GIF when FrontPage copies them to the Web page folder.

Figure 3-19 Clip Art Gallery

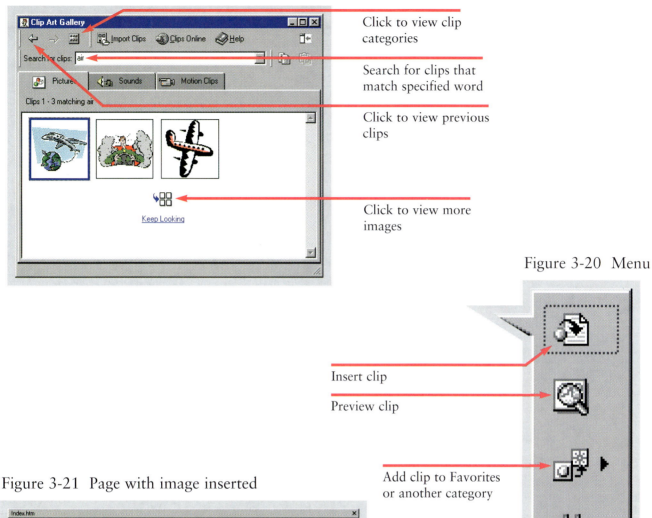

Click to view clip categories

Search for clips that match specified word

Click to view previous clips

Click to view more images

Figure 3-20 Menu

Insert clip

Preview clip

Add clip to Favorites or another category

Find similar clips

Figure 3-21 Page with image inserted

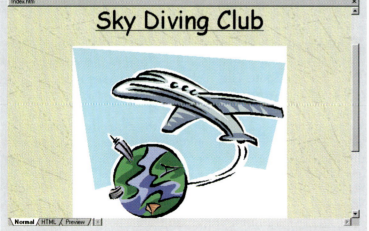

Practice

Insert an image into the **Index** page in the **Caddy Shop** Web. Insert it one line below the table. Search for a clip with the words **easy going**. Insert the clip on the left and save the file.

Hot Tip

To insert a picture you follow a similar procedure. Click **Insert**, then **Picture**, then **From File** on the submenu. You will just have to locate the picture file on your computer. Once you insert it, save the file in your Web.

Lesson 3 • Formatting and Adding Objects to Web Pages

Formatting Images

Concept

FrontPage gives you the ability to easily format images once they are placed on the page. After you place images on a Web page it is often necessary to resize them, change their location, or alter their colors. There are many different formatting effects that you can choose from.

Do It!

Sydney would like to resize the image in her Index page so that it is just a little bit smaller. She will also place a border around the image.

1. Open the Index page from the Skydiver Web.

2. Click the image to select it. Sizing handles appear at the corners and on each side of the image. Move the pointer over the sizing handle at the lower-right corner of the image. The pointer turns into a resizing arrow ↘.

3. Click and hold down the mouse button, drag it upwards until the entire table can be seen with the image, as shown in **Figure 3-22**.

4. Right-click the image. Click Picture Properties on the shortcut menu.

5. The Picture Properties dialog box opens. Click the Appearance tab. In the Border thickness: text box type 3, as shown in **Figure 3-23**.

6. Click [OK]. The image now has a border around it.

7. Save the changes.

More

Whenever you create a Web, FrontPage automatically creates an images folder. If you intend to use a lot of images, you should move them to this folder. Images can be saved there using the Save Embedded Files dialog box. This is a good file management practice that will allow you to quickly locate your images.

You can resize an image horizontally or vertically using the midpoint sizing handles. Clicking and dragging the right or left midpoint sizing handle will adjust the image horizontally, while dragging the top or bottom midpoint sizing handle will adjust it vertically. While the image is selected, you can delete it using the Delete key on the keyboard.

Formatting changes can also be made using the Image toolbar shown on page 3.23. The image can be rotated, flipped, cropped, beveled, and moved forwards or backwards. Text can be written over it, and contrast and brightness can be adjusted.

Figure 3-22 Resizing an image

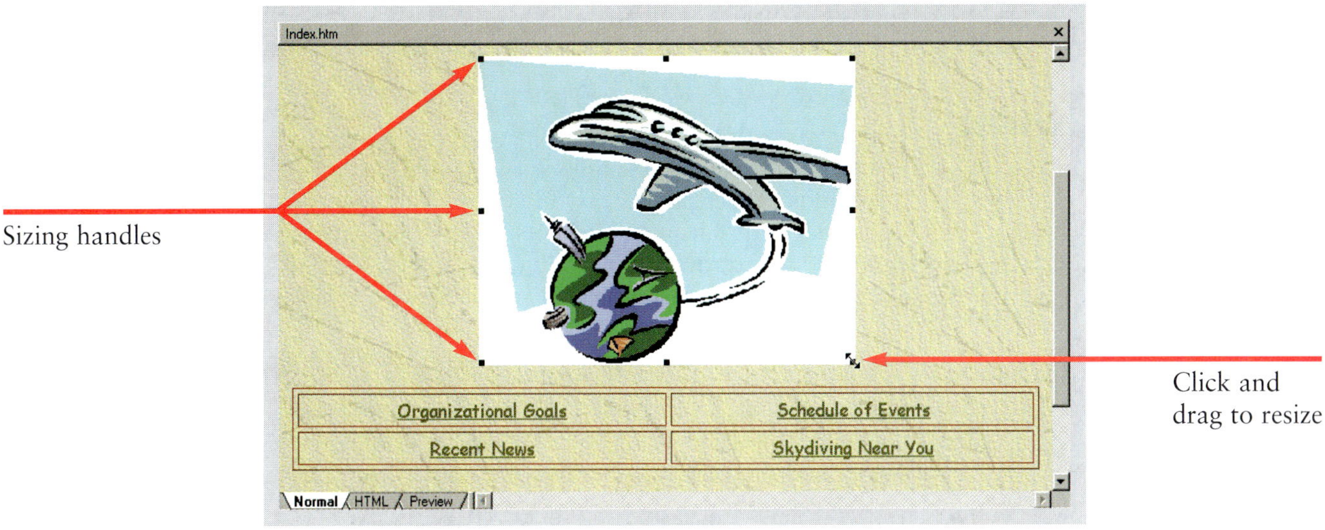

Sizing handles

Click and drag to resize

Figure 3-23 Picture Properties dialog box

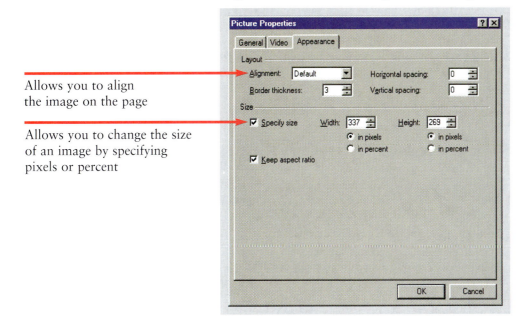

Allows you to align the image on the page

Allows you to change the size of an image by specifying pixels or percent

Practice

Resize the image on the **Index** page of the **Caddy Shop** Web so that it is larger, and centered.

Hot Tip

When you insert an image or click behind it, a large insertion point is placed behind the image. You can press the **Backspace** key to delete it or align it left, right, or center using the corresponding buttons on the **Formatting** toolbar.

Lesson 3 • Formatting and Adding Objects to Web Pages

Image Mapping

Concept

An image containing multiple links is called an image map. Creating a link between an image and another page is easy to accomplish. Image maps are also called clickable images or hotspots. Hotspots are invisible boxes on a picture, each of which has a link attached to it. The Image toolbar contains three buttons for creating differently shaped hotspots.

Do It!

Sydney is going to use the image she inserted to create a link to another page.

1. Open the Index page in the Skydiver Web.

2. Click the image to select it.

3. Click the rectangular hotspot button on the Image toolbar that appears at the bottom of the screen. The Image toolbar is shown in Figure 3-24.

4. Use the pointer, which is now a pencil to draw a rectangle around the airplane, as shown in Figure 3-25.

5. The Create Hyperlink dialog box opens. Click the link to new page button. It is the last of the four buttons to the right of the URL list box.

6. Select the Frequently Asked Questions page, the second icon in the second row of the New Page dialog box. Click OK.

7. Save the file under the default name, Table of Contents.

8. Open the Index page again.

9. Click the Preview tab. Notice that the pointer turns into a hand over the airplane as it would on any other hyperlink, but not when it is over part of the image that was not mapped, as shown in Figure 3-26.

10. Click on the image. The linked page opens.

11. Return to Normal view, and save the changes.

More

You can insert as many hotspots as will fit on an image, however, it is advisable to choose an image with easily distinguishable areas so that visitors can guess where the links are.

The entire image can also be a hyperlink. Simply click the image to select it and click Insert from the Menu bar. Then select Hyperlink and type in the URL, or locate the page or file you wish to link to in the Create Hyperlink dialog box.

To change a hotspot's link, double-click the hotspot and change the URL or find a new page or file to link to in the Edit Hyperlink dialog box. To delete a hotspot, click once to select it and press the Delete key.

Figure 3-24 Image toolbar

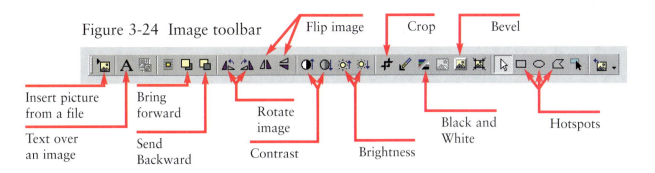

Insert picture from a file
Text over an image
Bring forward
Send Backward
Flip image
Rotate image
Contrast
Crop
Brightness
Bevel
Black and White
Hotspots

Figure 3-25 Creating a hotspot

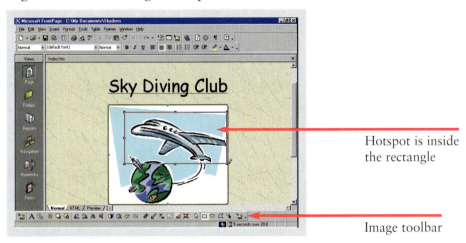

Hotspot is inside the rectangle

Image toolbar

Figure 3-26 A hotspot

Pointer over a hotspot

Practice

Create a hotspot on the **Index** page of the **Caddy Shop** Web. Link to a new **Frequently Asked Questions** page that you will create. Save everything.

Hot Tip

You can use the **Circular Hotspot** or the **Polygonal Hotspot** buttons on the Image toolbar to more precisely conform to the shape of the chosen area on the image.

Lesson 3 • Formatting and Adding Objects to Web Pages

Creating a Hover Button

Concept

A Hover button is one whose appearance changes when you pass the pointer or "hover" over it. It is a Java applet, which means that its special effects will appear only on browsers that can read the Java programming language. The button may glow, change color or even appear to bend inwards. Hover buttons are used as hyperlinks.

Do It!

Sydney is going to create a Hover button on one of her Web pages in the Skydiver Web.

1. Open the organizational_goals page, from the Skydiver Web.

2. Place the insertion point below the last line of text.

3. Click Insert, highlight Component and click Hover button from the submenu. The Hover Button Properties dialog box opens.

4. In the Button text: text box type Home.

5. Click [Browse...]. The Select Hover Button Hyperlink dialog box opens. Click the Index page to link to it, and click [OK].

6. Click the drop-down arrow in the Button color: list box. Choose the black square.

7. Click the drop-down arrow in the Effect color: list box. Choose the yellow square.

8. Click the drop-down arrow in the Effect: list box and select Reverse glow.

9. The Hover Button Properties dialog box should now look like Figure 3-27.

10. Click [OK].

11. Save the file.

12. Click the Preview tab.

13. Move the pointer over the Hover button, and it should glow, as shown in Figure 3-28. If you click on it, it will take you to the Index page.

More

If a visitor does not have a Java-enabled browser only the special effects will not function. The button will be present and the hyperlink will function, but the color change and glow will not occur.

Figure 3-27 Hover Button Properties dialog box

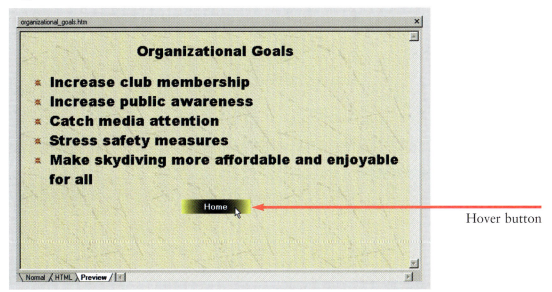

Basic button color

Changes the font on the button

Color that appears when pointer is over button

Figure 3-28 Hover button in Preview mode

Hover button

In the **Caddy Shop** Web, add a Hover button with special effects to the **table _of_ contents** page to link it to the **Index** page.

You can edit and make format changes to a Hover button by right-clicking it and selecting **Hover Button Properties** from the shortcut menu.

Lesson 3 • Formatting and Adding Objects to Web Pages

Creating a Marquee

Concept

A marquee is a piece of animated text. Marquees grab people's attention as they scroll across the Web page. Scrolling marquees are only supported by Internet Explorer. Visitors who use Netscape Navigator, will only see the marquee's text as ordinary text.

Do It!

Sydney is going to add a marque to the Index page in her Skydiver Web.

1. Open the Index page, in the Skydiver Web.

2. Place the insertion point in front of the S in Speed Demons.

3. Click Insert, highlight Component and click Marquee from the submenu.

4. The Marquee Properties dialog box opens. In the Text: text box type Come fly with us.

5. Click the Alternate radio button in the Behavior section, the The Marquee Properties dialog box is shown in Figure 3-29.

6. Click [OK].

7. Save the changes

8. Click the Preview tab.

9. The marquee moves around the screen, as shown in Figure 3-30.

More

Although marquees are typically placed at the top of a page they can be placed wherever you wish. If you place the insertion point at the end of a line of text, the marquee will be inserted on the following line. As you saw in the exercise above, if you place the insertion point before a line of text, the marquee will be inserted one line above it.

Figure 3-29 Marquee Properties dialog box

Controls the way the marquee moves

Speed in which marquee moves

Figure 3-30 Marquee sliding and scrolling across page

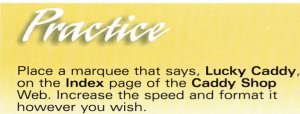

Marquee

Practice

Place a marquee that says, **Lucky Caddy**, on the **Index** page of the **Caddy Shop** Web. Increase the speed and format it however you wish.

Hot Tip

To format marquee text; click the marquee to select it. Sizing handles will surround the marquee. Either use the buttons on the Formatting toolbar, or click **Format** on the Menu bar and select **Font**, to open the **Font** dialog box.

Lesson 3 • Formatting and Adding Objects to Web Pages

Inserting Text Boxes

Concept

A text box is an area on a Web page where users can submit information back to the Web site. In FrontPage a text box is called a form field. Often users are asked to complete registration forms before they can use a Web site. You can create these forms with the Form Wizard. All forms contain a Submit and Reset button. After you insert a form onto your Web page, you must determine the what fields (or pieces of information) the visitor will be asked to submit.

Do It!

Sydney is going to add a form page to the Skydiver Web. Then she will begin adding form fields, by adding two one-line text boxes and a scrolling text box.

1. Open the Index page from the Skydiver Web.

2. Open a new, Normal page, by clicking File on the Menu bar, highlighting New and clicking Page from the submenu. When the New Page dialog box opens, click the Normal Page icon and click OK .

3. Press the [Enter] key three times.

4. Click Insert on the Menu bar, highlight Form and click Form from the submenu that appears. Two buttons appear. Place the insertion point in front of the Submit button and press the [Enter] key. Place the insertion point one line above the buttons and type Name. Then click Insert, highlight Form, and click One-Line Text Box from the submenu. The form is displayed in Figure 3-31. Press the [Enter] key.

5. Type e-mail address and insert another one-line text box. Press the [Enter] key.

6. Type, Describe your First Skydiving experience. Then click Insert, highlight Form, and click Scrolling Text Box from the submenu.

7. Save the changes. Use Form as the page title and save it as form.

8. Click the Preview tab. The form page should look like Figure 3-32.

More

To resize a text box, click it once to select it. Sizing handles will allow you to adjust its dimensions. If you right-click a text box you can access many formatting options from the shortcut pop-up menu.

FP 3.28

Figure 3-31 Form with text box inserted

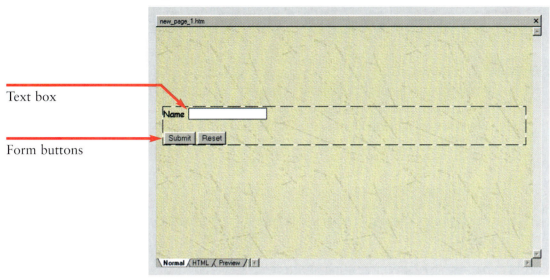

Text box

Form buttons

Figure 3-32 Text boxes in Preview mode

Text boxes are ready to be written in and submitted

Practice

Create a new form page in the **Caddy Shop** Web. Devise two short questions and create two one-line text boxes. Devise another question, with a lengthy answer, and insert a scrolling text box. Save the new page as **form** and change the title to **Form**.

Hot Tip

Click and drag a text box to reposition it in the form.

Lesson 3 • Formatting and Adding Objects to Web Pages

 Adding Check Boxes and Radio Buttons

Concept

Two other form fields are check boxes and radio buttons. Check boxes are used to submit yes or no answers. Radio buttons are generally created for questions where the answers are limited to several options. These two form fields facilitate data entry by allowing visitors to answer questions with a click of the mouse.

Do It!

Sydney is going to add a check box and radio buttons to her Form page.

1. Open the Form page in the Skydiver Web.

2. Place the insertion point before the Name text box. Press the [Enter] key.

3. Place the insertion point one line above the Name text box.

4. Type Check the box if you have gone skydiving before.

5. Click Insert on the Menu bar, highlight Form and click Check Box from the submenu. A check box is inserted, as shown in Figure 3-33.

6. Press the [Enter] key.

7. Type: If so how many times?:. Press the [Enter] key again.

8. Click Insert, highlight Form, and click Radio Button from the submenu. A radio button is inserted. Type: 1-10, then press [Tab]. Add another radio button. Type 11-20. Press [Tab]. Add another radio button, type 21 and over.

9. Save the changes.

10. Click the Preview tab. Your page should look like Figure 3-34.

More

Radio buttons and check boxes are similar in that visitors can choose from one or more options. Radio buttons offer a group of options from which one is chosen. Check boxes are generally used to answer yes or no questions but can also be created in situations where you want to allow multiple selections. Radio buttons and check boxes cannot be resized or reshaped.

Figure 3-33 Form page with check box

Check box

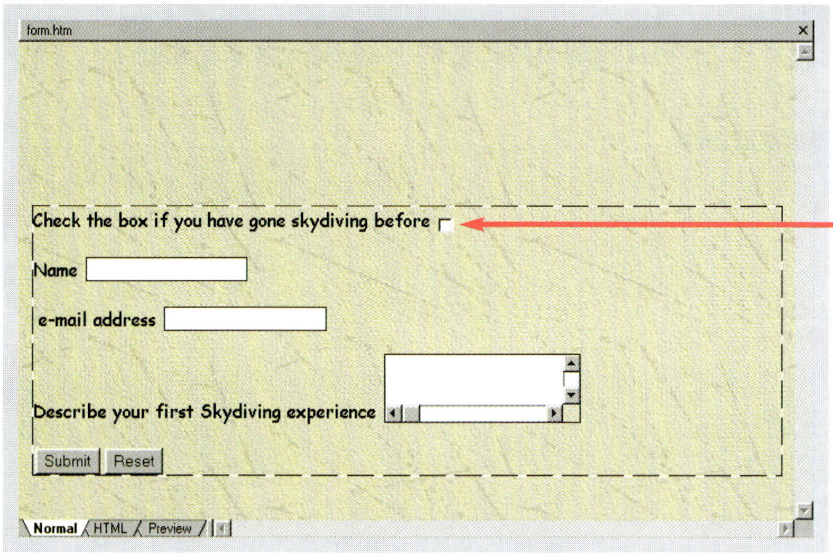

Figure 3-34 Form page with radio buttons

Radio buttons

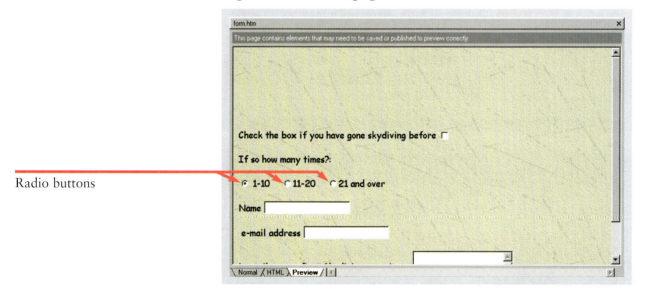

Practice

Compose a yes or no question and add it, along with a check box, to the **Caddy Shop** Web **form** page. Insert an option group with 2-3 radio buttons.

Hot Tip

The **Form Page Wizard** can also construct radio buttons. If you enter a list in the **Enter the Labels for the Options** text box, a group of radio buttons will be created.

Lesson 3 • Formatting and Adding Objects to Web Pages

Creating a Drop-Down Menu

Concept

Another form field that can be created is a drop-down menu. After creating a drop-down menu, you must add the selections from which the visitor will choose. Drop-down menus are used when there are multiple selections. They simplify data entry and save space on the form.

Do It!

Sydney will now add a drop-down menu to the form that she has been working on.

1. Open the Form page from the Skydiver Web.

2. Place the insertion point after the scrolling text box.

3. Press the [Enter] key.

4. Type: What area of the country do you live in?.

5. Click Insert on the Menu bar. Highlight Form and click Drop-Down Menu from the submenu.

6. Double-click the drop-down menu. The Drop-Down Menu Properties dialog box opens.

7. Click [Add]. The Add Choice dialog box opens. Type: Northeast, as shown in Figure 3-35. Click [OK]. In the Initial State section, make sure the Not selected radio button is selected.

8. Follow the same procedure to add Southeast, Midwest, South, Sunbelt, Rockies, North, Northwest, and West Coast. In the Name: text box type Area. When you are finished the dialog box should look like Figure 3-36.

9. In the Allow multiple selections section, make sure the radio button next to No is selected. Click [OK]. Save the changes.

10. Click the Preview tab. When you click the drop-down arrow, the menu should appear, as shown in Figure 3-37.

More

In the example above, we left Not selected as the initial state for each radio button. If you think most visitors will choose a particular answer however, you can make one of the options appear preselected. If the user would have chosen that option, he or she can skip that field. They can select another option if the initial state is incorrect.

You can edit your entries using the Modify button [Modify...] in the Drop-Down Menu Properties dialog box. You can rearrange the list order using [Move Up] and [Move Down]. An option is also available for permitting visitors to make multiple selections from the list. Since this is not generally done however, this could be confusing to visitors. Check boxes are probably a better choice when you want to allow multiple selections. [Remove] enables you to delete entries.

FP 3.32

Figure 3-35 Add Choice dialog box

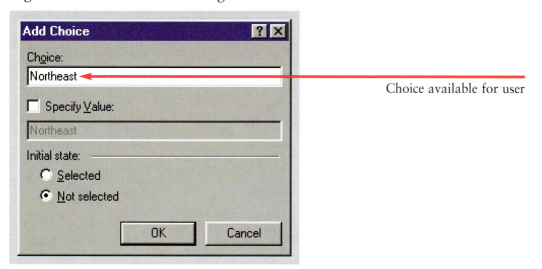

Choice available for user

Figure 3-36 Drop-Down Menu Properties dialog box

List of choices that will be available on menu

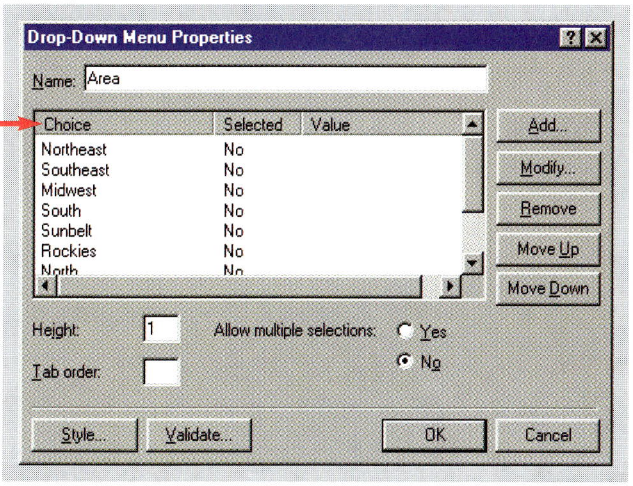

Figure 3-37 Drop-Down Menu

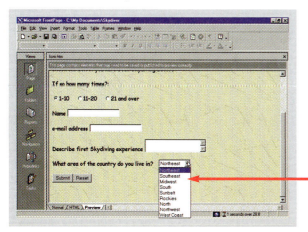

Drop-down menu created to your specifications

Practice

Create a drop-down menu of payment methods on the **form** page of the **Caddy Shop** Web. Your list should include: **cash, credit card, debit card, cash on delivery,** and **money order**.

Hot Tip

Click [Validate...] to set data entry rules for the drop-down menu. You can stop a form from being submitted unless a menu item is selected, or you can disallow certain items from being selected. These options are available on all form controls.

Lesson 3 • Formatting and Adding Objects to Web Pages

Creating a Push Button

Concept

Another form field is a push button. Most Web authors leave the Reset and Submit buttons at the bottom of the form page. However, sometimes it may be convenient to locate a Reset or a Submit button at some earlier point in the form. In these cases a push button can be it inserted. A push buttons can also be used to answer a yes or no question.

Do It!

Sydney is going to create a button that will Reset the form, so users don't have to scroll to the bottom of the form if they want to reset it.

1. Place the insertion point after the check box at the top of the form.
2. Press the [Tab] key five times.
3. Click Insert, highlight Form and click Push Button from the submenu. The button is created in the location you specified.
4. Double-click the button. The Push Button Properties dialog box opens.
5. In the Value/label: text box type Reset.
6. Click the Reset radio button to the right of Button type:.
7. The Push Button Properties dialog box should now look like Figure 3-38.
8. Click OK.
9. Save the changes.
10. Click the Preview tab. Your form should now look like Figure 3-39.

More

To specify where a form is going to be submitted, right-click Submit. Then click Form Properties from the shortcut menu. Use the Form Properties dialog box to locate a file or folder to send completed forms to, or an e-mail address where completed forms will be sent. You can also send forms to databases or to other types of files for storing data.

FP 3.34

Figure 3-38 Push Button Properties dialog box

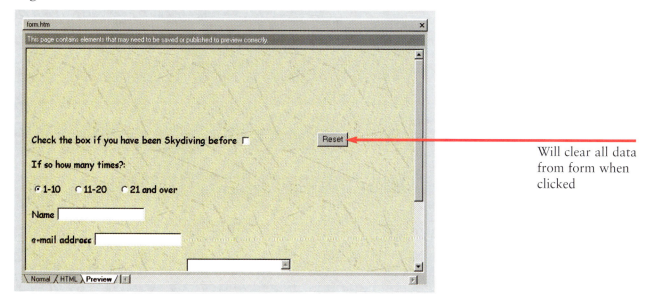

Normal button may be used to enter data, like a check box

Figure 3-39 Button in a form

Will clear all data from form when clicked

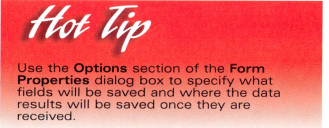

Practice

Add a **Reset** button somewhere on the **Form** page in the **Caddy Shop** Web.

Hot Tip

Use the **Options** section of the **Form Properties** dialog box to specify what fields will be saved and where the data results will be saved once they are received.

Shortcuts

Function	Button/Mouse	Menu	Keyboard
Bold	B		[Ctrl]+B
Italics	I		[Ctrl]+I
Underline	U		[Ctrl]+U
Center			[Ctrl]+E
Align left			[Ctrl]+L
Align right			[Ctrl]+R
Hyperlink		Click Insert, then click Hyperlink	[Ctrl]+K
Insert picture from file		Click Insert, highlight Picture, then click From File	
Insert table		Click Table, highlight Insert, then click Table	
Bullets and numbering		Click Format, then click Bullets and Numbering	
Font	A	Click Format, then click Font	
Theme		Click Format, then click Theme	
Decrease indents			[Ctrl]+[Shift]+M
Increase indents			[Ctrl]+M

INTERACTIVE COMPUTING • FrontPage 2000

Identify Key Features

Name the items indicated by callouts in **Figure 3-40**.

Figure 3-40 Formatted Web page

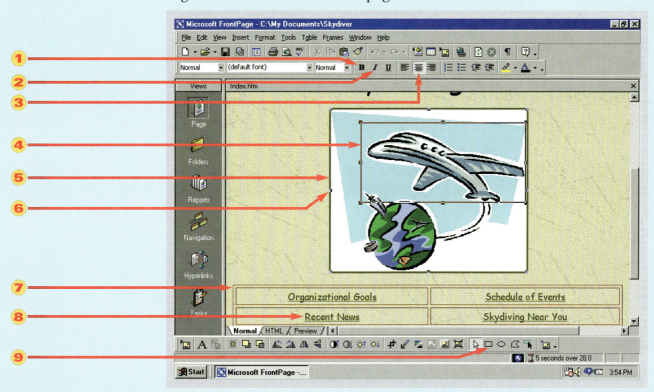

Select The Best Answer

10. Formats an entire Web with similar fonts, color schemes, and other formatting options
11. Organizes information in a structured and attractive way
12. Creates a hyperlink over a specific area of an image
13. Creates a title for a page that scrolls or slides across the screen
14. Form field used for a yes or no question
15. Controls the typeface style
16. The hotspot button is found here
17. The bold and italic buttons are found here
18. A button that creates an effect when the mouse moves over it

a. hotspot
b. Font list box
c. Marquee
d. Formatting toolbar
e. Image toolbar
f. Hover button
g. Table
h. Theme
i. Check box

FP 3.37

Lesson 3 • Formatting and Adding Objects to Web Pages

Quiz (continued)

Complete the Statement

19. When you move the pointer over the screen to enter text the pointer turns into an:
    a. I-beam
    b. Insertion point
    c. I-point
    d. Insertion beam

20. You can change the properties of a numbered or bulleted list by:
    a. Double-clicking the list
    b. Right-clicking the list and selecting List Item Properties from the shortcut menu
    c. Right-clicking the list and selecting Number and Bullet Properties from the shortcut menu
    d. Double-clicking the list and selecting List Properties from the shortcut menu

21. To figure out how many rows and columns you need to create a certain number of cells:
    a. Add the number of rows plus the number of columns
    b. Subtract the number of columns from the number of rows
    c. Multiply the number of rows by the number of columns
    d. Multiply the number of cells you need by the columns, then divide by the number of rows

22. You can perform every function from the Create Hyperlink dialog box except:
    a. Color the hyperlink
    b. Link to a new page
    c. Create a link that sends an e-mail
    d. Search the browser for a page to link to

23. The most efficient file formats for saving large images are:
    a. RIFF
    b. JIFF and TIFF
    c. GIF and JPEG
    d. PREG and FREG

24. A hyperlink over a specified area of an image is also called a:
    a. Linked map
    b. Warmspot
    c. Coolspot
    d. Hotspot

25. A Java applet, which is used to create a hover button is:
    a. Named after a type of fruit
    b. Designed to run on every browser no matter what
    c. A set of instructions written in the Java language
    d. Utterly useless without a plug in

26. An alternative method of creating radio buttons is:
    a. Using the Corporate Presence Wizard
    b. Using the Form Page Wizard
    c. Using the Submit Form Template
    d. With the Radio Button Properties dialog box

Interactivity

Test Your Skills

1. Create and format a list:

   a. Open the **Water Taxi** Web.

   b. Create a new blank page in the Web, save it as, and title it **Locations**.

   c. Create a bulleted list for the water taxi destinations: **Ocean Harbor**, **Lee Beach**, **Red Sands**, **Bay Sands**, **Cherry Road**, **Blue Birch**, and **Tom's Grand Cove**.

   d. Change the font of the list text and save the page.

2. Insert a table:

   a. Create a new page called **Fees**. Save it in the **Water Taxi** Web.

   b. Insert a table to organize the destinations listed above and their associated fees: **$3.50**, **$6.25**, **$4.75**, **$10.00**, **$5.25**, **$2.50**, and **$8.25** respectively.

   c. Save the page.

3. Apply a theme to a Web:

   a. In the **Water Taxi** Web, apply the **Rice Paper** theme to the entire Web.

   b. Design a custom theme using the **Sumi Painting** theme. Name the new theme, **Customized theme**.

   c. Apply the custom theme to the entire Web.

4. Create Hyperlinks:

   a. Create hyperlinks from the already existing text on the **Index** page of the **Water Taxi** Web. Create the new pages to which they will link. For example, create a link from the **Fees** link in the table to the newly created **Fees** page. Create a link from the **Information** link on the Index page to the newly created **Locations** page.

   b. For the rest of the links in the table, link them to a new page titled and saved with the same name as the link. Create a **Staff** page, an **Employment** page, a **Weather** page, and a **Related Services** page.

   c. Test all the links to make sure they work.

5. Add an image and create a hotspot:

   a. Create a new page, save it as, and title it **Image**. Save it in the **Water Taxi** Web.

   b. Search the **Clip Art Gallery** using the word **water**. Select and insert the clip of the boat on the right.

   c. Create a hotspot somewhere on the image that links it to a new form page that you will create using the **Form Page Wizard**. Save and title the page **Form**.

Interactivity (continued)

Test Your Skills

6. Create a hover button and a marquee:

    a. Open the Index page from the Water Taxi Web.

    b. Create a scrolling marquee for the company name.

    c. Open the Information page.

    d. Create a hover button with special effects that links to the Index page in the Water Taxi Web.

7. Add form fields to the Water Taxi Web form page:

    a. Open the Form page in the Water Taxi Web.

    b. Add a check box at the top of the form that asks, Would you like to make reservations for a water taxi ride?.

    c. Type: How many people will be joining you?. Create three radio buttons for the options: 1-4, 5-8, and 9-12 people, with one radio button for each option.

    d. Next type: On what date will you be riding with us?. Add a one-line text box after the question.

    e. Type: How did you hear about us?, and add a scrolling text box to the page.

    f. Type: Where will you be going to?. Create a drop-down menu that includes the list of locations that you entered on the Information page earlier.

Problem Solving

You have been doing a good job at Diggs & Associates but the tough part has just begun. You must now format the Web to meet the tastes and the organizational needs of your employers. Insert a table with hyperlinks to each page in the Web. For example, create a cell that says, Products and Services and link it to the Products and Services page. Design a conservative, professional-looking theme to apply to the Web. The Bold Stripes and Industrial themes are good places to start. Customize one of these two themes if you so desire. On the Products and Services page, create a products list including the categories: Fiction, Non-Fiction, How-To, Textbooks, Poetry, Drama, Biographies, Reference, and Childrens. Create a marquee for the company name. At the bottom of the page create a Hover button with the special effects and colors of your choice. Be sure to save after reformatting or adding objects to a page. Save the pages in the Diggs Web.

Interactivity (continued)

Problem Solving

Create a form page using the **Form Page Wizard**. Select, **ordering information** as the type of input to collect. Save the results to a text file. Keep the rest of the default settings. Add a one-line text box labeled, **Name:** Insert a scrolling text box so users can describe how they heard of Diggs & Associates. Provide a check box for next day delivery. Create three radio buttons to identify new customers, customers who have previously ordered from Diggs, and customers who have not ordered in a year. Create a drop-down menu list of Diggs' products that have been purchased before. Include, **None** for new customers.

Begin formatting your personal Web site. You may want to begin by writing and formatting text. Change the font to set the tone for your site. Apply **bold** formatting, or **underline** or **italicize** your text. Align it left, right or center. If you have digital camera photographs, or are able to scan photos, you can add these to your site. You can create text hyperlinks, image hyperlinks and/or hotspots. You can create an image map to link to the other pages in your Web. If appropriate, organize information into a table or create a numbered or bulleted list. Decide if you want Hover buttons or a marquee for your Home page. Get out the list you created earlier and insert the elements you found appealing.

Create a form page either from scratch or using the **Form Page Wizard**. If you use the Wizard, you must determine what information to extract from the visitor. There are several types of inputs you can collect to get personal data. You can create radio buttons or check boxes. If you do not use the Wizard, determine what information you want to gather and compose your questions. Create the appropriate form fields for each question. Some questions may require text boxes and others a drop-down menu. When you are finished, save the page as, **form** and title it, **Form**.

- Creating a Web Hierarchy
- Adding a Navigation Bar
- Viewing and Printing the Web Structure
- Organizing Files in Folders View
- Verifying Hyperlinks
- Renaming Pages and Changing URL's
- Opening an Office Document in a Web
- Using the Office Clipboard
- Publishing a Web

PUBLISHING AND MAINTAINING WEB PAGES

After you have designed and formatted your Web, you must maintain it. Hyperlinks can be broken, components may be malfunctioning, or new links may need to be created. Web site maintenance includes checking components, verifying that hyperlinks are targeted to the correct locations, and ensuring that visitors can easily navigate the site.

Other basic tasks you need to learn are how to import Office documents, and how to use the Office clipboard. FrontPage Web pages can be created quickly using a word processing program such as Word, with which you may be more familiar. Entire documents can be inserted, or portions of documents can be cut and pasted onto a Web page.

After you have previewed and tested your Web, it will finally be time to publish it. Viewing it over the Internet is after all, the final goal. Updating your Web after a period of time is as easy as publishing it.

Case Study:
Sydney is going to check the Speed Demons Web to verify that all the components and hyperlinks are operational. She will add Navigation bars to produce an easily navigable layout. She will also organize her files, rename a page, and change a URL. Finally, she will use FrontPage to publish her Web site so that all of its elements can be viewed over the Internet.

Lesson 4 • Publishing and Maintaining Web Pages

Creating a Web Hierarchy

Concept

Creating a Web hierarchy will help you to organize your links. When the structure or hierarchy of your site has been defined, FrontPage will be able to create Navigation bars to connect the Web pages. A Web hierarchy, also called a tree diagram, is created in Navigation view. When you create a Web using a Web Wizard the tree diagram will be automatically constructed.

Do It!

Sydney is going to use Navigation view to create a Web hierarchy or tree diagram for her Skydiver Web site.

1. Open the Index page in the Skydiver Web.

2. Click the Navigation button on the Views bar. The Navigation view should resemble Figure 4-1. The Navigation view shows the Speed Demons page, or the Index page, and a list of files on the left called the Folder List.

3. In the Folder List, click and drag the organizational_goals file so that it is underneath the Speed Demons page. When you release the mouse button, the organizational_goals page is linked to the Index page as shown in Figure 4-2. The Organizational Goals page is now a child page of the Index page.

4. Next Click and drag the news page so it is underneath the Index page and next to the Organizational Goals page. It is thus a child page of the Index page and on the same level as the Organizational Goals page.

5. Follow the same procedure until the Local, Table of Contents, and Form pages are all child pages of the Index page.

6. Finally click and drag the calendar page so that it is underneath the News page. Thus the Calendar page will be a child page of the News page. The tree diagram or Web hierarchy is shown in Figure 4-3.

More

A Web hierarchy organizes the links in a Web. It is a prerequisite to creating Navigation bars. Navigation bars are rows of buttons or text that link to the other pages in the Web. Following the tree diagram, Navigation bars will be created to link the parent page, Index, to every other page except the Calendar page. Conversely, each of the child pages will link back to the Index page. The Calendar page will link to its parent page, News.

Most Web pages have lowercase file names. Lowercase names refer to files, while uppercase names refer to page titles. Notice that the file names in the Folder List are lowercase and the page titles in Navigation view are uppercase.

To reorganize the tree, click and drag a page to a different position in the hierarchy. Observe the line that appears as you drag, and position the page to create the desired relationship. There is no need to save a hierarchy. FrontPage will reopen a Web with the last tree diagram you created before exiting the program.

Figure 4-1 Page in Navigation view

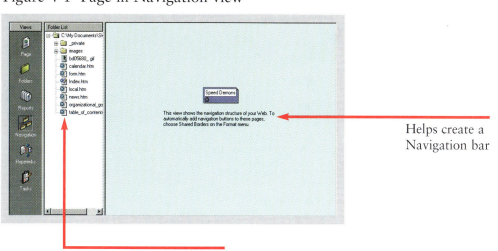

Helps create a Navigation bar

List of folders and files in the Web

Figure 4-2 Home page and child page

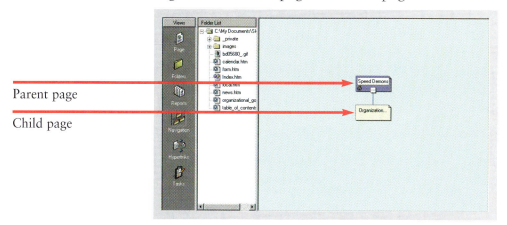

Parent page

Child page

Figure 4-3 Web hierarchy

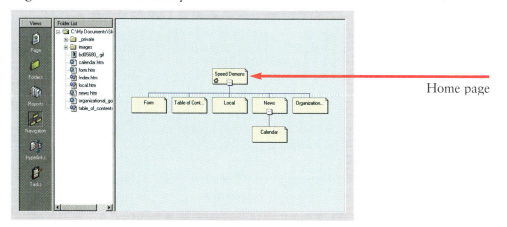

Home page

Practice

Create a hierarchy so that the **Employment**, **Best Selling Items**, **Form**, and **Sales** pages are child pages of the **Index** page. Make the **Table of Contents** page a child page of the **Best Selling Items** page.

Hot Tip

If you create a form page and save the results to a text file, it will be included in the **Folder List**. Do not add it to the hierarchy. It will still be part of the Web.

Lesson 4 • Publishing and Maintaining Web Pages

Adding a Navigation Bar

Concept

Navigation bars are rows of text or buttons that allow you to navigate through a Web. When you create Navigation bars, the links behind them are automatically produced. Navigation bars can be formatted to enhance Web site attractiveness.

Do It!

Sydney is going to add Navigation bars.

1. Open the **Index** page of the **Skydiver** Web.

2. Click the **Navigation** button on the **Views** bar. The hierarchy appears in **Navigation** view.

3. Click **Format** on the Menu bar, you may have to access the extended menu. then click **Shared Borders**. The **Shared Borders** dialog box opens.

4. Make sure the **All pages** radio button is selected.

5. Click the **Left** check box, then click the **Include navigation buttons** check box. The dialog box should now look like **Figure 4-4**.

6. Click **OK**. Click the **Page** view button on the **Views** bar. Hyperlinks appear on the left of the **Index** page. When you move the pointer over one of these links it turns into.

7. Double-click one of the links. The **Navigation Bar Properties** dialog box opens.

8. Make sure that the **Child level** radio button is clicked. Also make sure that the **Home Page** and **Parent Page** check boxes are checked.

9. Check the **Buttons** radio button in the **Orientation and appearance** section, so that your dialog box looks like **Figure 4-5**.

10. Click **OK**. Click the **Preview** tab. Your page should look like **Figure 4-6**.

11. Save the changes. A **Save As** dialog box will open to save the shared borders in a new folder in the Web called **Borders**.

More

You can test the Navigation bars by previewing the Web in a browser. After opening the Web in your browser, click the Navigation bars to verify that the target pages open.

Not all pages will link to each other. The child pages of the **Index** page link back to their parent, **Home**, which is the **Index** page. The **News** page links to its parent page, **Index**, and its child page, **Calendar**.

A Navigation bar can also be inserted by clicking Insert from the Menu bar and selecting the Navigation Bar command. The properties are then set in the **Navigation Bar Properties** dialog box.

FP 4.4

Figure 4-4 Shared Borders dialog box

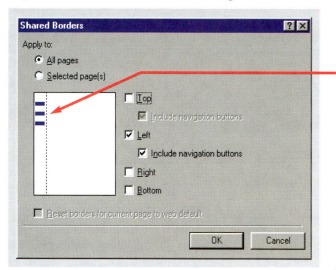

Preview of where the Navigation bar will appear

Figure 4-5 Navigation Bar Properties dialog box

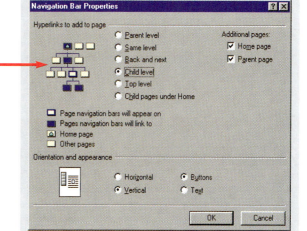

Preview of which pages contain which hyperlinks

Figure 4-6 Page with Navigation bar

Navigation bar with buttons and links specified in earlier dialog boxes

Practice

Create a Navigation bar in the **Caddy Shop** Web. Make it a horizontal bar and use text links rather than buttons. Save the changes.

Hot Tip

After they have been clicked, hyperlinks change color. Hyperlink text colors can be modified by accessing the **Background** dialog box from the **Format** menu. You cannot access this feature however, if a theme is applied.

Lesson 4 • Publishing and Maintaining Web Pages

Viewing and Printing the Web Structure

Concept

When you are in the process of designing a Web, having a hard copy of the site structure can sometimes be useful. If you are creating a site for someone else, an outline of the proposed structure can demonstrate the progress you are making, or serve as a visual aid in presentations. FrontPage enables you to print the tree diagram directly from Navigation view.

Do It!

Sydney is going to view her hierarchy in Navigation view and print a hard copy.

1. Open the Index page of the Skydiver Web.

2. Click the Navigation button on the Views bar.

3. Click the white box at the bottom of the Speed Demons page in Navigation view. The hierarchy collapses, as shown in **Figure 4-7**.

4. Click the new box to expand the hierarchy.

5. Click File on the Menu bar, then click Print.

6. The Print dialog box opens, as shown in **Figure 4-8**.

7. Make sure you have the correct printer selected. Then click OK.

8. A copy of the navigation structure should print.

9. Exit the application. Save any changes to the print settings you might have made.

More

The Print Preview command is also found on the File menu. You may have to access the expanded menu to find it. The Print Preview command enables you to view the tree diagram, as it will look when printed. Once you know its parameters, you can make the necessary changes to ensure that it prints properly. You can change the page orientation to Landscape, in the Features tab of the Print dialog box, using the Properties button. This may be necessary to ensure that it fits on one page. You can also return to Page view and select the Page Setup command from the File menu. The margins can be adjusted in the Print Page Setup dialog box. Orientation and paper size can also be altered in the Print Page Setup dialog box using the Options button.

FP 4.6

Figure 4-7 Web hierarchy collapsed

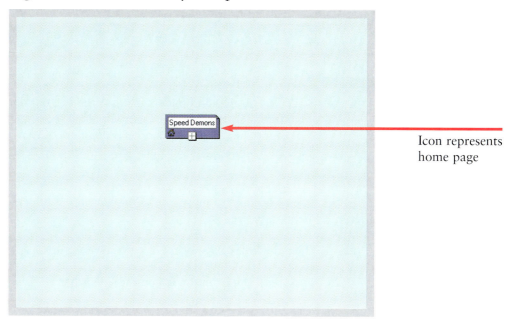

Figure 4-8 Print dialog box

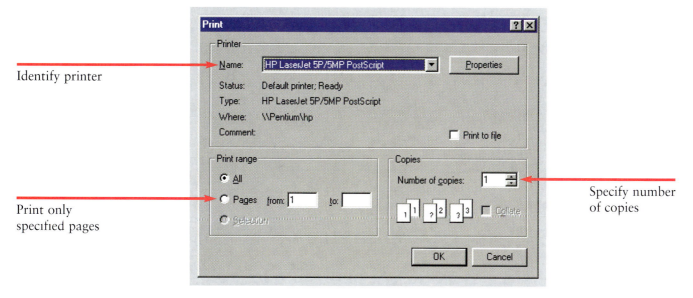

Practice

Print two copies of the navigation structure of the **Caddy Shop** Web.

Hot Tip

Click **Properties**, in the **Print** dialog box, to change everything from page orientation to graphical resolution.

Lesson 4 • Publishing and Maintaining Web Pages

Organizing Files in Folders View

Concept

As additional files and folders increase the size of your Web, some basic organizational skills become essential. Some file organization can be done in Navigation view, but the majority is done in Folders view. These basic skills include moving, renaming, and sorting files.

Do It!

Sydney is going to move one of the files into a folder, rename another file, and sort the files by size.

1. Open the Index page of the Skydiver Web.

2. Click the Folders button on the Views bar.

3. Click and drag the bd05680_.gif image file from the Contents window of the screen to the images folder in the Folder List section of the screen, as shown in Figure 4-9.

4. Right-click the file fphover.class. This is one of the Hover button files. Click Rename from the shortcut menu.

5. The name of the text becomes highlighted. Type hoverbutton.class, and press the [Enter] key. A warning dialog box appears, asking you if they should update the hyperlinks affected by the name change, as shown in Figure 4-10. Click Yes.

6. Click the title heading Size in the Contents window, click the title. The files will be sorted in ascending size order, as shown in Figure 4-11. Click it again and the files will be sorted in descending size order.

7. Save the changes.

More

You can view and modify file properties by right-clicking a file, and selecting Properties from the shortcut menu. The Properties dialog box allows you to change page titles, view the size and modification dates of files, add comments to the file, and assign the file to a workgroup.

Figure 4-9 Folders view

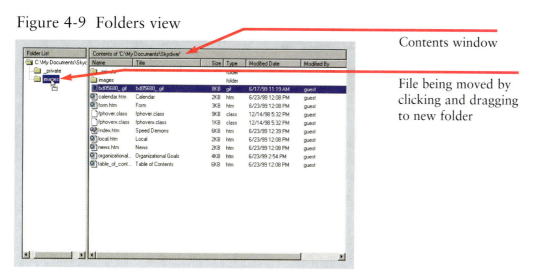

Contents window

File being moved by clicking and dragging to new folder

Figure 4-10 Rename warning dialog box

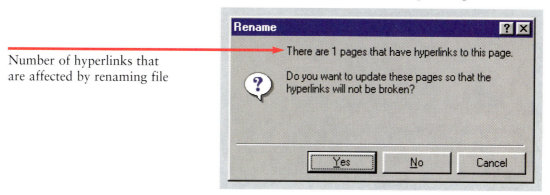

Number of hyperlinks that are affected by renaming file

Figure 4-11 Files sorted by size

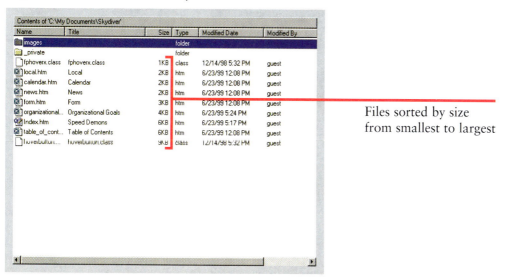

Files sorted by size from smallest to largest

Practice

In the **Caddy Shop** Web, rename the image file you inserted earlier to **caddy.gif**. Then move it to the **images** folder. Finally, sort the files by the **Modified Date**.

Hot Tip

To view the contents of a folder in the **Folder List**, click the plus sign  next to that folder.

Lesson 4 • Publishing and Maintaining Web Pages

Verifying Hyperlinks

Concept

Hyperlinks are one of the most important elements in a Web. If hyperlinks are malfunctioning, Web visitors will be unable to navigate the site. A broken hyperlink may disallow a user from viewing the page they require. Incorrect target names, changed file names, or a changed or incorrect URL's can cause broken hyperlinks. There are several ways to verify hyperlinks. Earlier, we tested them in a browser. Now, we will use Reports view and Hyperlinks view to verify hyperlinks.

Do It!

Sydney is going to make sure that all of the hyperlinks in her Web are working properly.

1. Open the Index page in the Skydiver Web.

2. Click the Reports button on the Views bar.

3. The Site Summary opens, as shown in Figure 4-12.

4. Notice that the summary reveals no broken hyperlinks. It does however, reveal one unlinked file. Double-click the Unlinked files row in the Site Summary.

5. The file that is unlinked is fphoverx.class. It is an important Hover button file, so you do not need to make any changes to it.

6. Click the Hyperlinks button on the Views bar. An icon for the file you were just looking at appears unlinked on the screen.

7. Click the Index page in the Folder List. All of the hyperlinks to and from the Index page are displayed, as shown in Figure 4-13. Links to the page you are viewing appear on the left, and links from that page appear on the right.

8. Click the News page from the Folder List. There are two links from the Index page and one link from the Calendar page. The News page links to the Index page and the Calendar page.

More

Hyperlinks can be repaired manually by opening the pages containing the faulty hyperlinks and either repairing or deleting them. They can be repaired using the Recalculate Hyperlinks command in the Tools menu. The Recalculate Hyperlinks dialog box informs you that the command will repair the hyperlinks in your Web, update the components, including shared borders and Navigation bars, and synchronize Web data.

Figure 4-12 Reports view

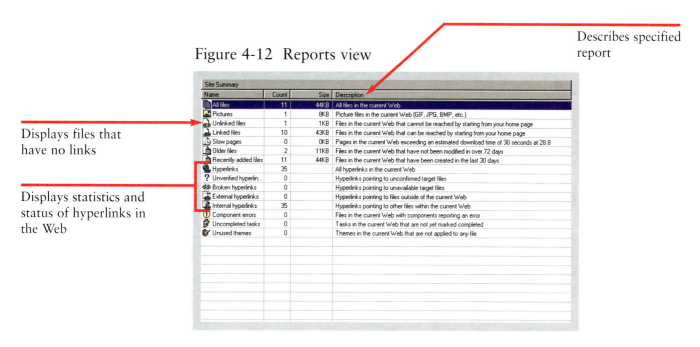

Describes specified report

Displays files that have no links

Displays statistics and status of hyperlinks in the Web

Figure 4-13 Hyperlinks view

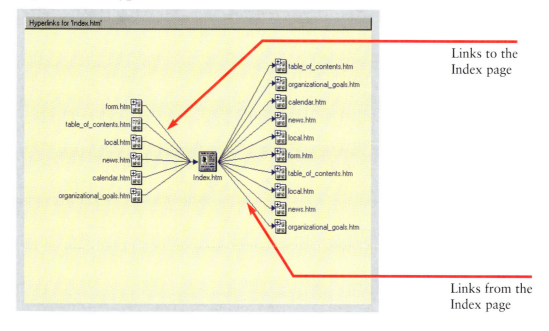

Links to the Index page

Links from the Index page

Verify that all of the hyperlinks in the **Caddy Shop** Web are functional. Repair them if necessary.

Hot Tip

Clicking the plus sign in the upper-left corner of the page icon in **Hyperlinks** view expands the diagram. The left side displays the links to that page, and the right side displays links from that page.

Lesson 4 • Publishing and Maintaining Web Pages

Renaming Pages and Changing URL's

Concept

Two other important file management tasks are renaming pages and changing URL's. Earlier we changed the file name of a page but not its title. In this skill we will change the page title and the URL. Distinctive titles are important for both the Web author and the Web site visitor. If page names are too similar, distinguishing between them can become problematic. In the sample Web, a second form page should be given a distinctive title so that the Web designer does not make errors creating links and the Web site visitor is able to navigate to the correct page.

Do It!

Sydney is going to rename and change the URL of one of the pages in her Skydiver Web.

1. Open the Index page in the Skydiver Web.
2. Click the Navigation button on the Views bar.
3. Right-click the Speed Demons page icon, click Rename from the shortcut menu.
4. The title is highlighted. Type Home, and press the [Enter] key.
5. Right-click the Index page in the Folder List, and click Rename from the shortcut menu.
6. The file name is highlighted. Type home.htm. Press the [Enter] key. Click Yes in the Rename dialog box to update the pages so that links will not be broken.
7. Right-click the Home page icon again. Click Properties from the shortcut menu. The Properties dialog box should look like **Figure 4-14**.
8. In Navigation view the Home page should now look like **Figure 4-15**.
9. Return to Page view and save the changes.

More

You can also change the URL in Page view. Right-click an empty area on the page and click Page Properties from the shortcut menu. Type the desired URL in the Base location: text box in the Page Properties dialog box. This is not neccessary in the exercise above because changing the file name will change the URL.

You should check Reports view after changing a URL to verify that no hyperlinks were broken.

If you save a file under a new name, the old file will still exist. If the file is not deleted, it can disrupt file management. Both file names will be in your Folder List and you may accidentally create a link to the obsolete version.

FP 4.12

Figure 4-14 Properties dialog box

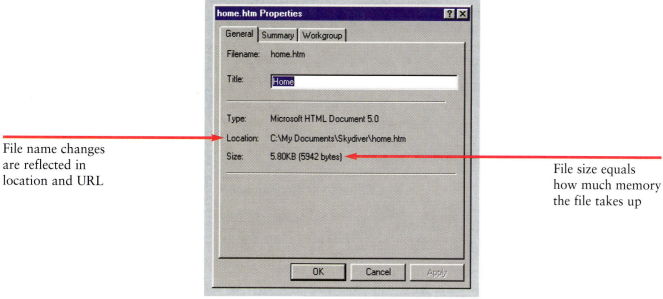

File name changes are reflected in location and URL

File size equals how much memory the file takes up

Figure 4-15 Change reflected in Navigation view

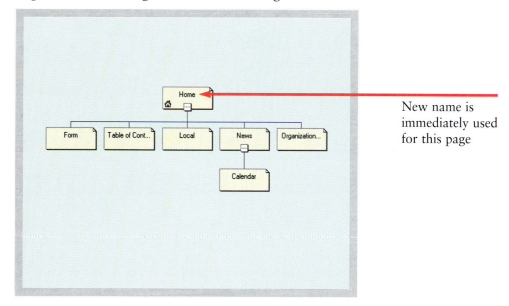

New name is immediately used for this page

Practice

Change the title and file name of the **Index** page in the **Caddy Shop** Web to **Home**, and **home.htm** respectively.

Hot Tip

You can access the **Rename** and **Properties** commands to make changes to the **URL** or page title, by right-clicking the file icon, or the page icon, in any of the different FrontPage views.

Lesson 4 • Publishing and Maintaining Web Pages

Opening an Office Document in a Web

Concept Many Microsoft Office programs allow you to save documents in HTML format and open pages in your default browser. Office documents can be imported and published in a Web. Almost all Microsoft created documents can be imported into a FrontPage Web.

Do It! Sydney will demonstrate to her colleagues how to open an office document in FrontPage.

1. Open Microsoft FrontPage. Do not open any Webs, begin with a blank page.

2. Click Insert, then click File. The Select File dialog box opens.

3. Click the Files of type: drop-down list and click Word 97-2000 (*.doc), as shown in Figure 4-16.

4. Locate your Student Files folder.

5. Locate and click document Doit4-9.

6. Click **Open**. You may have to install this feature from your Office 2000 CD-ROM.

7. The Word document opens, as shown in Figure 4-17.

8. Save the page in My Documents as wordfile.

More You may have noticed when you accessed the Files of type: drop-down list, that Word documents are not the only files that can be inserted into a Web Page. You can insert Rich Text Format (RTF) documents, Plain text (TXT or ASCII) files, Excel worksheets, or Lotus1-2-3 worksheets, WordPerfect 5.x and 6.x, Works 4.0, Word for Macintosh, and HTML documents.

Instead of cutting and pasting, or reentering data, importing allows you to take previously saved documents in various formats and convert them to HTML.

Figure 4-16 Select File dialog box

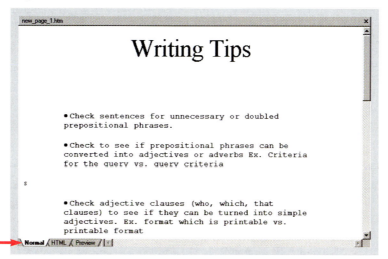

Lists the formats that can be inserted into FrontPage Webs

Figure 4-17 Word document

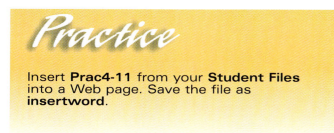

Page can be viewed in all three formats

Practice

Insert **Prac4-11** from your **Student Files** into a Web page. Save the file as **insertword**.

Hot Tip

When the document opens in FrontPage, it has been converted to HTML and is now a Web document.

Lesson 4 • Publishing and Maintaining Web Pages

Using the Office Clipboard

Concept

The Office clipboard is a new feature of Office 2000. It enables you to save up to twelve pieces of data from any Office program to the clipboard. Clipboard items can be pasted into other programs or used within a single application. Data is sent to the clipboard using the Cut and Copy commands. After it is saved to the clipboard, the Paste command is used to insert it into the various programs.

Do It!

Sydney is going to copy and paste data from one program to FrontPage with the aid of the Office Clipboard.

1. Locate your Student Files folder and open Doit 4-13.

2. Microsoft Word opens to a meeting agenda. Click View on the Menu bar, highlight Toolbars and click Clipboard from the submenu. The Office Clipboard opens.

3. Scroll down the document until you reach the Agenda section of the document. Highlight the entire Agenda section beginning with Ad Campaign and ending with State of the Club.

4. Click Edit on the Menu bar, then click Copy. That section of the text is sent to the Office Clipboard, as shown in Figure 4-18.

5. Close Microsoft Word. You may be asked if you want data on the clipboard to be available for use in other programs, if so click [Yes].

6. Open FrontPage, and open the News page from the Skydiver Web.

7. Type Monthly Meeting Agenda. Press the [Enter] key.

8. Click Edit on the Menu bar, then click Paste.

9. Save the changes. This page should now look like Figure 4-19.

More

There is also a Paste Special command on the Edit menu, you may have to access the extended menu to reach it. The Paste Special command on the expanded Edit menu enables you to paste data onto the clipboard in different formats. You can create one paragraph, break it into several paragraphs, turn it into formatted paragraphs, add line breaks, or simply treat the data as HTML.

The Office Clipboard can not be viewed in FrontPage.

Using the Office clipboard, you can copy and paste the portions of a document you need, rather than importing the entire document.

FP 4.16

Figure 4-18 Office Clipboard

Data copied from Word

Purges the clipboard of all data

Figure 4-19 Data pasted into FrontPage

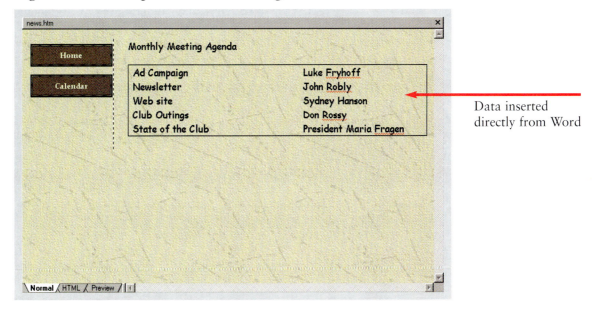

Data inserted directly from Word

Open **Prac4-15**. There is only one line of text. Copy it from Word and paste it at the bottom of the **Home** page in the **Caddy Shop** Web.

Hot Tip

You can also cut, copy and paste data within the FrontPage program. If you place something incorrectly, or put it on the wrong Web page, you can cut it and paste it to the correct location.

Lesson 4 • Publishing and Maintaining Web Pages

Publishing a Web

Concept

When you create a Web site, the goal is to get it published. You can publish directly to a Web server using FrontPage. New pages can be published and existing ones can be changed with ease. If you find mistakes, or have a page that requires continuous updating, just edit your original files and republish. The changed files will automatically replace the existing ones.

Do It!

Sydney is going to publish her Web so that it can be viewed as a Web site.

1. Open Doit4-17 in FrontPage from your Student Files folder. Save it as table_of_contents in your Skydiver Web. When a dialog box asks you if you want to replace the file of the same name, click [Yes].

2. Click File, on the Menu bar and click Publish Web, you may have to access the extended menu to find the Publish Web command. The Publish Web dialog box opens.

3. Click [Options ▼].

4. In the Specify the location to publish your web to: text box type C:/My Documents/Published Skydiver Web. Make sure the Publish all pages radio button is selected, as shown in Figure 4-20. Click [Publish].

5. A dialog box will open telling you that one of the components on your pages will not work unless it is copied to a Web server with FrontPage extensions installed. Click [Continue].

6. The files begin copying to the neccessary folder, as shown in Figure 4-21.

7. When it finishes a dialog box opens telling you that your Web has been published successfully, as shown in Figure 4-22.

8. Click the link to view the published Web. All the objects and all the links should work properly now that the Web is published.

9. Close the browser, and click [Done], then close FrontPage.

More

Before you publish your Web with a server, you will need several pieces of information. You will need to get the address of your Web server, and an assigned name for your Home page. You will also need to find out if they have FrontPage extensions. In some cases, in order to be viewed, components require that your Web server have this special Microsoft software installed. If your Web server does not have FrontPage extensions, you may be able to get the address of an FTP, or File Transfer Protocol, server to circumvent this problem. Your Web server will also give you folder information, such as, what folder they want you to upload to, and how they want your Web files to be organized. Once you have published the Web, you can publish individual pages, or the entire Web again to continually update it.

Figure 4-20 Publish Web dialog box

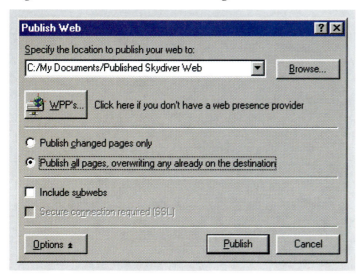

Figure 4-21 Publishing a Web

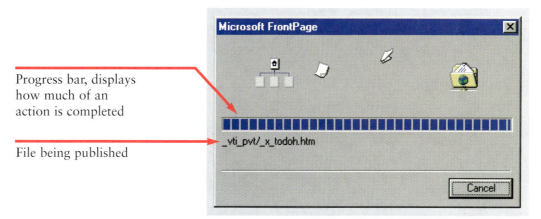

Progress bar, displays how much of an action is completed

File being published

Figure 4-22 A Web published successfully

Link to new published Web site

Practice

Publish the **Caddy Shop** Web to **C:/My Documents/Caddy Shop Web Final**.

Hot Tip

Many Web servers require you to join their online communities and choose a user name and password. You will be required to enter them when you publish your Web.

Lesson 4 • Publishing and Maintaining Web Pages

Shortcuts

Function	Button/Mouse	Menu	Keyboard
Copy		Click Edit, then click Copy	[Ctrl]+C
Cut		Click Edit, then click Cut	[Ctrl]+X
Paste		Click Edit, then click Paste	[Ctrl]+V
Folder List		Click View, then click Folder List	
Print		Click File, then click Print	[Ctrl]+P
Publish Web		Click File, then click Publish Web	[Alt]+P
Page View		Click View, then click Page	
Folders View		Click View, then click Folders	
Reports View		Click View, then click Reports	
Navigation View		Click View, then click Navigation	
Hyperlinks View		Click View, then click Hyperlinks	
Tasks View		Click View, then click Tasks	

INTERACTIVE COMPUTING • FrontPage 2000

Identify Key Features

Name the items indicated by callouts in Figure 4-23

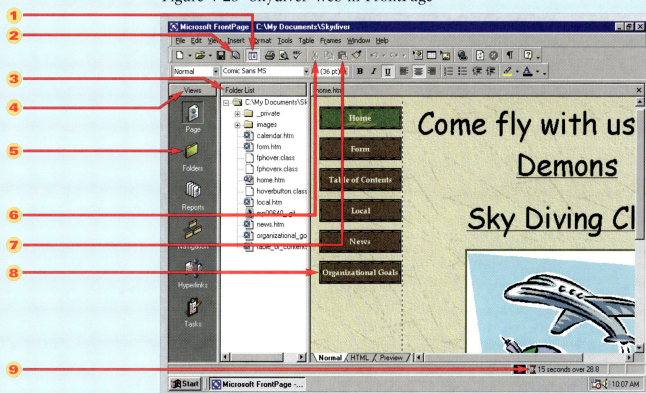

Figure 4-23 Skydiver Web in FrontPage

Select The Best Answer

10. A Web hierarchy is also known as
11. You can add a Navigation bar to your Web pages using this command
12. A printed reproduction of a computer screen
13. When your hyperlinks are broken use this command
14. A Web address
15. What view should you use to make sure that all your files and links work properly
16. This holds up to twelve pieces of data
17. Access this menu to open an Office document in FrontPage
18. Allows you to view what a page will look like when it is printed

a. Shared Borders
b. Reports
c. Office Clipboard
d. Recalculate hyperlinks
e. Insert
f. Hard copy
g. Print Preview
h. Tree diagram
i. URL

FP 4.21

Quiz (continued)

Complete the Statement

19. You must use this view to create a Web hierarchy:
    a. Reports
    b. Hyperlinks
    c. Tasks
    d. Navigation

20. A list of files and folders appears in:
    a. Tasks view
    b. Folder List
    c. Reports view
    d. Hyperlinks view

21. When you insert a file from another program you must use this dialog box:
    a. Insert Document
    b. Select File
    c. Insert Data
    d. Insert

22. To prevent people from sabotaging sites that are not theirs, most Web servers require:
    a. A user name and password
    b. A computer ID number
    c. A coded entry language
    d. A keyword or secret phrase

23. One method you can use to format hyperlinks is to access:
    a. The Hyperlinks menu
    b. The Background dialog box
    c. The Foreground dialog box
    d. The Page Properties dialog box

24. You can use these two commands to take data from one document and insert it into another:
    a. Copy and Insert
    b. Cut and Insert
    c. Cut and Place
    d. Copy and Paste

25. Once an Office document has been opened in FrontPage it is converted to:
    a. FrontPage speak
    b. Java
    c. HTML
    d. Applet

26. Clicking the plus sign, in Navigation view and Hyperlinks view, performs this function:
    a. Expands the diagrams
    b. Contracts the diagrams
    c. Expands the menu
    d. Contracts the window

Interactivity

Test Your Skills

1. Create a Web hierarchy:

   a. Open the **Water Taxi** Web.

   b. Switch to **Navigation** view. Click and drag files from the Folder List so that they are child pages of the **Index** page.

   c. Make the **Form** page in the **Water Taxi** Web a child page of the **Fees** page.

2. Create a Navigation bar:

   a. Create a Navigation bar on the **Index** page that links to all of its child pages.

   b. Make sure there is a link from the child pages back to the **Index** page.

   c. Also make sure there is a link from the **Fees** page to the **Form** page.

   d. Make the links in the Navigation bar **text** rather then buttons.

3. Print the Web structure:

   a. Open the **Water Taxi** Web in **Navigation** view.

   b. Print the structure of the Web.

4. Verify your hyperlinks:

   a. Open the **Water Taxi** Web in **Reports** view.

   b. If there are broken hyperlinks, repair them with the **Recalculate Hyperlinks** command.

   c. Make sure that files that need to be linked are linked.

   d. View the Web in **Hyperlinks** view to make sure all of the pages are linked properly.

5. Open an Office document in a Web:

   a. Open **Test 4** in FrontPage.

   b. Save it as **Resume**.

6. Publish a Web:

   a. Open the **Water Taxi** Web.

   b. Publish the Web to **C:/My Documents/Watertaxiweb**.

   c. After it is published, view the Web.

Interactivity (continued)

Problem Solving

Your work at Diggs & Associates is almost finished. Your job does not include composing all the text. You are to train a group of Diggs employees to finish creating and maintain the site. They will complete any additional pages following the design, theme, color scheme, and style you have devised. Before you are finished, you must create a Web hierarchy, and Navigation bars. The Index page, of course, will be at the top of your hierarchy. The **Search**, **Feedback**, **Contents** and all other pages will be child pages of the **Index** page. After you have completed the tree diagram, create Navigation bars. Use button hyperlinks for your Navigation bars. They should link from the **Index** page to each child page, according to the hierarchy you created. Each child page should in turn, link back to the Index page. Demonstrate your progress to Diggs' executives by printing several copies of your Web structure. View the Web in Folders view and if necessary, move image files to the image folder and rename files.

Verify the hyperlinks in the Diggs Web. First view the Web in **Reports** view. Make sure none of the neccessary files are unlinked. Also make sure there are no broken hyperlinks. If any of the hyperlinks are broken use the Recalculate hyperlinks command to fix them. Rename all of the pages so that thy are easier to organize. Rename any similarly titled pages. For example, the Services pages need distinct names rather than **Service 1**, **Service 2**, etc. This will enable Diggs' employees to locate particular pages for editing. Finally publish the Web to **C:/My Documents/Diggsweb**.

Continue working on your personal Web. First, create a Web hierarchy. If you used a wizard to create your personal Web, this was done automatically. If you added pages to a Home page, or formatted several pages and linked them together however, you will need to either edit or create a tree diagram. If you decide to add Navigation bars, make sure they complement your chosen style. Print the Web structure and view the Web in **Folders** view. Reorganize files and folders if necessary.

View the Web in **Reports** and **Hyperlinks** views to verify the hyperlinks. Thoroughly navigate your Web as a final check that all links are functional. Make sure all file names, URL's and page names are correct. If you want to put poetry or fiction that you have written, or a resume, on your site, import the documents from your word processing program. If you promote it, prospective employers or publishers might discover and view your Web site. Use the Office Clipboard to insert a table, or a block of text from another program. Remember to save imported documents and make sure they are linked to your site. Finally, publish the Web. If you have a URL and a Web server, and are confident that your site is ready, you can publish it with your Web server. If not, publish it to **C:/My Documents/(file name)**, as we did in the lesson.

Glossary

A

Align left, right
Command buttons on the Formatting toolbar that change the alignment of the text on a Web page by aligning the text to the left or the right side of the page.

Answer Wizard
A part of the FrontPage Help feature, it allows you to type a question, and will search for the help topics that might be useful in answering that question.

Applet
A set of instructions written in Java that tells your browser how to interpret a certain object and effect, it only works with Java enabled browsers.

B

Background
A command on the Format menu that allows you to make formatting changes to different aspects of Web pages.

Bold
A command button on the Formatting toolbar that makes the selected text appear in bold lettering.

Broken hyperlink
A hyperlink that has a target page that does not exist, has been moved, or changed, or for some other reason the hyperlink does not work, or link to an appropriate file.

Browser
See Web Browser.

Bulleted list
A type of list in which the information is organized by graphical marks, called bullets, representing a new section of information on the list.

C

Cell
The empty spaces that are created by the rows and columns of a table. Contains the information in a table.

Center
A command button on the Formatting toolbar that changes the alignment of the text on a Web page by aligning it in the center of the page.

Check box
A check box is another way of answering a yes or no question, the user has an option of checking the box to select it, a yes answer, or not checking it, a no answer.

Child page
A page, in a Web hierarcy, which appears below another page in the hierarchy, and therefore can only be linked to from that page.

Click
To press and release a mouse button in one motion; usually refers to the left mouse button.

Clickable image
Another name for a hotspot or an image map, an image that is formatted so that a hyperlink is added to a particular place on the image. When clicked this spot acts as a hyperlink.

Clip Art Gallery
A gallery of images that Microsoft provides that you can search and use to add graphics to your Web pages.

Close button
A sizing button that appears on the Title bar, when clicked it closes the application.

Column
The vertical border of a table, that intersects with the rows to make up the empty spaces of the table called cells.

Contents
A part of the FrontPage Help feature, this allows you to search for help based on a table of contents with help topics that you can choose to look at.

Control
An object that makes data entry easier and more efficient, most controls appear on form pages, such as check boxes, and radio buttons.

Control Menu icon
An icon that appears in the Title bar that opens a menu, when clicked, that allows you to manipulate the FrontPage window.

Copy
A command found on the Edit menu that copies the selected text and moves it to the Office Clipboard.

Cut
A command found on the Edit menu that cuts the selected text and moves it to the Office Clipboard.

D

Decrease indents
A command button on the Formatting toolbar that allows you to decrease the indentation between the text and the margins.

Desktop
The standard Microsoft Windows screen, it is designed to have the appearance of an actual desktop.

Dialog Box
A box that groups functions together, it performs certain actions depending on the commands you use and the options you select.

Drag
To hold the mouse button down while moving the mouse.

Drop-Down arrow
An arrow that appears in a text box, clicking it opens up a menu of options to choose from.

Drop-Down Menu
A menu of options that opens by clicking the drop-down arrow. You can also use FrontPage to create a drop-down menu on a form page.

E

Edit
A menu on the Menu bar that provides you with commands that allow you to make changes, edit, your Web and Web pages.

F

File
A menu on the menu bar, it provides commands that have to do with saving, opening, printing, storing, and performing other filing options on your Web and Web pages.

Find
A command found on the Edit menu, searches for text that you specify and takes you to where the text is located on a page, or in a Web.

Folder List
A list of files and folders that appears to the left of the FrontPage screen, it can also be accessed by opening the View menu.

Folders View
Allows you to view and organize the folders and files that are associated with a Web.

Font
The style in which text appears. Bold, italic, script, serif, and sans serif are all styles associated with different fonts.

Form page
A type of Web page that asks the user for information, once the information has been entered the page may be sent to the Web manager, and saved, or sent to an e-mail address so the data can be recorded.

Format
A menu on the Menu bar that allows you to make formatting changes to your Web and Web pages.

Formatting
The process of adding elements to your Web page, including objects, text, colors, and other important Web components to give your Web a certain look or style, and make it attractive.

Formatting toolbar
A bar full of buttons and icons that allows you to perform certain formatting actions on your Web pages.

Frames
A menu on the Menu bar that allows you to add frames to a page, create a frames page, and make changes to frame pages.

G

Graphic Interchange Format (GIF)
A format in which images are saved, where the image is compressed so that it does not take up much space, and doesn't take long to download.

H

Help
A Microsoft feature that provides several different ways of searching for help and information while you are using a Microsoft program. You can access this feature with the Help menu on the Menu bar.

Home page
The first page that a visitor sees when they enter your Web site. It is where they begin to navigate through your Web.

Hotspot
Another name for an image map or a clickable image, when an image is formatted so that a particular spot on the image is linked to a target page. When clicked the hotspot acts as a hyperlink.

Hover button
A button added to a Web page which creates an effect when the pointer hovers over it, the button is actually a Java applet.

Hyperlink
A hyperlink is a piece of text that links to another page inside the Web, or externally to another Web altogether.

Hyperlinks View
Displays every hyperlink to and from each page in a Web.

Hypertext Markup Language (HTML)
A code used for designing Web pages. FrontPage writes HTML code for you, but a knowledgable user may also write HTML code for a page in FrontPage.

HTML tab
Found in Page view, this mode of viewing a page allows you to look at and edit the HTML code that makes up the Web page.

I

I-beam
When you move the mouse pointer over text or an area of a page where text may be inserted it turns into an I-beam so named because it looks like an I-beam.

Icon
A small graphic that identifies an object or a button.

Image map
Another name for a hotspot or clickable image, when an image is formatted so that a particular spot on the image is linked to a target page. When clicked the spot acts as a hyperlink.

Image toolbar
A bar containing buttons that perform specific actions when clicked, this particular toolbar contains command buttons that act on images alone.

Increase indents
A command button on the Formatting toolbar that allows you to increase the indent between the text and the margins.

Index
A part of the FrontPage Help feature, this function allows you to get help by typing a keyword and searching for the help topics related to that keyword.

Insert
A menu on the Menu bar that allows you to insert certain objects and files into your Webs and Web pages.

Insertion point
A flashing point on a page, it marks the point where text will be entered on the page, or where an object will be placed.

Internet
A global network of computers exchanging information over the network, it includes the Web servers, the individual user, and organizations that manage the networks.

Italic
A command button on the Formatting toolbar that makes the selected text appear italicized.

J

Java
A Web designing language. Similar to HTML, Java is read by browsers and then used to display Web pages, but Java allows certain effects to be created which are not possible in HTML.

Java applet
A set of instructions written in the Java language which tells the browser which effects to perform when the page is displayed. These applets are only visible with Java enabled browsers.

Joint Photographic Experts Group (JPEG)
A format in which images are saved, where the image is compressed so that it does not take up much space, and doesn't take long to download.

K

Keyword
A part of the Index help feature, type in a keyword and the help feature will find a help topic related to that keyword.

L

List
A list is a way of organizing information on a Web page by displaying it in list format.

Lotus 1-2-3
A spreadsheet program, using FrontPage you can open documents from this program and put them on a Web page.

M

Marquee
An object that takes text and moves it accross the screen to grab the viewers attention.

Maximize button
A sizing button found on the Title bar that maximizes the size of the FrontPage window.

Menu
A list of related commands.

Menu bar
Found below the Title bar, it contains the names of menus that present lists of commands to choose from.

Minimize button
A sizing button the Title bar that minimizes the size of the FrontPage window so that it no longer appears on the screen.

Mouse pointer
The arrow shaped cursor on the screen that you control by guiding the mouse on your desk. You use the mouse to select and drag items, choose commands, and start or exit programs. The shape of the mouse pointer can change depending on the task being executed.

N

Navigation bar
A group of hyperlinks appearing as buttons or simply as text which guide a user through the navigation of your Web, by providing hyperlinks, internally, to pages in the Web.

Navigation button
A button that links to other pages to help navigate a user through a Web.

Navigation View
Displays the navigation structure of a Web. It also allows you to add Navigation buttons and a Navigation bar to your pages.

New Page
A command found on the File menu that allows you to create a new page with a template, a wizard, or just a blank page.

New Web
A commad found on the File menu that allows you to create a Web using a template, a Wizard or a simple one-page Web.

Normal Tab
Found in Page view, this mode of viewing a page allows you to add objects and elements, and perform some of the formatting options available to you in FrontPage.

Numbered list
A type of list in which the information is organized by numbers representing a new section of information on the list.

O

Office Clipboard
Allows you to send up to 12 pieces of data from programs to the clipboard, by cutting or copying, then allows you to take data off the clipboard and use it in other programs.

Open File
A command found on the File menu that allows you to open any previously saved file.

Open Web
A command found on the Menu bar that allows you to open any previously saved Web.

P

Page View
This view allows you to work on an individual Web page. Most of the formatting, adding elements, and graphics to a Web page is done in this mode.

Parent page
The page that appears above another page in the Web hierarchy, so that it links to the child page.

Paste
A command found on the Edit menu that allows you to take data from the clipboard and paste it in a document.

Plain Text (TXT or ASCII)
A format that data appears in. It is significant because you can use FrontPage to open data in this format and place it on a Web page.

Preview in Browser
A command found on the File menu, it allows you to open your Web in a browser, you may use any browser that is used by your computer.

Preview Tab
Found in Page View, this mode of viewing a page allows you to see what the page would look like if it were published on the internet and viewed with a browser.

Print
A command found on the File menu that allows you to print a copy of the FrontPage screen, so that you can have a hard copy of the pages that will be published.

Print Preview
A view that shows how an object will appear when printed on paper. Useful for evaluating the layout or structure of a Web, before publishing it.

Publish Web
A command found on the File menu that publishes your Web to a Web server or to another location that you specify.

Push button
A button that is added to a form page that allows a user to submit a form or to reset a form, these options may be set when the button is created.

R

Radio button
A group of buttons that allows the user to select one or more of several options. Users may be allowed to select more than one, or can be limited to only one selection, out of several radio buttons.

Recalculate Hyperlinks
A command found on the Tools menu that fixes broken hyperlinks, by locating the intended target pages.

Recent File
A command found on the File menu that allows you to instantly open one of the most recent files you have been working on.

Recent Web
A command found on the File menu that allows you to instantly open one of the most recent Webs you have been working on.

Rename
A command found on many shortcut menus that allows you to rename an object using the Rename dialog box.

Replace
A command found on the Edit menu, it is related to the Find command. It allows you to find information on a page or in a Web and replace it with the text you specify.

Reports View
Provides reports and updates on the status of the files and hyperlinks of a Web, so you can keep it up to date.

Resizing arrow
When the pointer is moved over an object and you have the option of resizing it, the pointer will turn into an arrow, clicking and dragging the arrow will resize the object.

Restore button
A sizing button found on the Title bar that allows you to revert the FrontPage window to its previous size.

Rich Text Format (RTF)
A format in which data sometimes appears, FrontPage can open a document in this format and place it on a Web page in HTML format.

Right-click
To click the right mouse button; often used to access specialized menus and shortcuts.

Row
The horizontal border of a table, it intersects with columns to create the empty spaces called cells.

S

Save
A command found on the File menu that saves a file simply by overwriting the existing saved document.

Save As
A command found on the File menu that allows you to save a file with a new name and a new location.

Scroll arrow
Arrows that appear on the right and bottom of the FrontPage screen, they allow you to scroll through a document one line at a time, by clicking the arrow in the direction you want to the view to move.

Scroll bar
A graphical device for moving vertically or horizontally through the FrontPage screen with the mouse. Scroll bars are located along the right and bottom edges of the FrontPage window.

Scroll bar box
A small grey box located inside a scroll bar that indicates your current position relative to the rest of the window. You can advance a scroll bar box by dragging it, or by clicking the scroll arrows.

Shared Borders
A command found on the Format menu that allows you to add a Navigation bar to a Web, this is most useful when you add the shared borders in Navigation view.

Shortcut key
A keyboard equivalent of a menu command such as [Ctrl]+[S] for Save.

Shortcut menu
A pop-up menu accessed by right-clicking the mouse. The contents of the menu depend on your current activity.

Site Summary
A type of report provided in Reports view that evaluates files, folders, and hyperlinks to make sure that every element of your Web is kept up to date.

Sizing buttons
Three buttons found on the Title bar that allow you to manipulate the size of the FrontPage window.

Sizing handles
The small black squares that appear on the border of an object when it is selected. Dragging these handles will allow you to resize the object.

Spelling Checker
A command found on the Tools menu, it checks the spelling of words on a page or in a Web with the words in its internal dictionary.

Standard toolbar
Found below the Menu bar, it contains graphical buttons that execute specific commands.

Status Bar
Appears at the bottom of the screen and displays the activity being performed, as well as displaying currently active features, including the loading time for a Web page.

Style box
A box on the Formatting toolbar that allows you to set and change the style of text that appears in a Web page.

T

Table
An object that you can insert into a Web page to help organizing information. The table is made up of rows and columns which create cells, the cells contain the information. The Table menu on the Menu bar is used to insert and format tables.

Target
The page, Web, or location that a hyperlink links to. When creating a hyperlink the target page or URL must be specified. The target page must also be in working order for the hyperlink to work.

Tasks View
Displays the tasks that are and must be completed in a Web.

Template
A basic structure or outline that FrontPage provides you with to help you start your Web. The pages may include placeholder text which you simply overwrite to create your page.

Text box
A box that appears on a form page that allows users to enter text into it, a one-line box allows a short entries, while scrolling text boxes allow longer entries.

Theme
An overall style or look that is applied to a Web page or an entire Web, it is customizable so you can create your own.

Title bar
Contains the application Control menu icon, name of the application, and sizing buttons, it appears at the very top of the FrontPage screen.

Toolbar
A graphical bar containing buttons that act as shortcuts for common commands.

Tools
A menu on the Menu bar that allows you to select options that are useful for setting the technical properties of the FrontPage screen, Webs, and Web pages.

Tree diagram
Another name for a Web hierarchy, it is the basic structure of a Web displaying all parent and child pages and their relationships to one another.

U

Underline
A command button on the Formatting toolbar that makes the selected text underlined.

Uniform Resource Location (URL)
The address of a Web page. Every page has its own URL, no two URL's are exactly the same.

V

View
A menu on the Menu bar that allows you to choose certain ways of viewing your Web and Web pages, and allows you to manipulate what tools and toolbars are visible.

Views bar
The bar of buttons found on the left side of the FrontPage screen. This is where you find the View buttons that allow you to perform different functions in a Web.

View buttons
Found on the Views bar, these buttons allow you to control the way you view a Web, and allow you to perform different functions in a Web.

W

Warning
A dialog box that opens to ensure that you are performing the action that you want, you can continue the action, or cancel it. It is used to prevent you from losing data or making irreversible changes that you don't want to make.

Web
An assortment of Web pages that make up a Web site.

Web Browser
A program that has the abiltity to display Web pages, and can access them off of the Internet, it displays pages by reading the code they are written in.

Web Hierarchy
Another name for a tree diagram, it is the basic structure of a Web displaying all parent and child pages and their relationships to one another.

Web Page
A document that appears on the Internet with its own URL. It may contain graphics, text, or any number of elements that may be viewed once it is published.

Web Server
Is a computer running software that stores Web pages and objects, so that when a browser requests a page or object, the server furnishes the request, the browser interprets the objects as pages, text, graphics, etc.

Web site
Is made up of one or more Web pages that are linked and may be navigated by a visitor. Web sites are managed and owned by a person, company, or an organization.

What's This
A help feature that allows you to point to an object on the screen, a small box will open describing what that object is.

Window
A menu on the Menu bar that allows you to manipulate the FrontPage window. Also a rectangular area on the screen where you view and work on files.

Windows Taskbar
Usually located at the bottom of your screen, it contains buttons that allow you to open programs and perform certain functions.

Wizard

A wizard is a series of dialog boxes that allows you to enter data and choose options and uses those choices to create a page or a Web for you, based on your specifications.

Word

A Microsoft program that is used for word processing, you can use FrontPage to open a document from Word on a Web page.

WordPerfect

A word processing program, FrontPage can open this document and place it on a Web page.

Index

A

Align left, FP 3.4-3.5
Align right, FP 3.2
Answer Wizard, FP 1.14-1.15
Applet, FP 3.24-3.25
Applying themes, FP 3.10-3.11

B

Bold, FP 3.2
Broken hyperlinks, FP 4.10
Browser: see Web browser
  previewing Web page in, FP 2.18-2.19
Bulleted lists, FP 3.4-3.5

C

Cell Properties, FP 3.8-3.9
Cells, FP 3.6-3.9
Centering, FP 3.4-3.5
Check boxes, FP 3.30-3.31
Child pages, FP 4.2-4.3
Clickable image, FP 3.22-3.23
Clip Art Gallery, FP 3.18-3.19
Close button, FP 1.7
Color Wheel, FP 3.12
Columns, FP 3.8
Component menu, FP 3.24-3.27
Contents, FP 1.14-1.15
Control menu icon, FP 1.6-1.7
Controls, FP 3.30-3.31
Copy, FP 4.16-4.17
Corporate Presence Wizard, FP 2.6-2.9

Creating:
  drop-down menus, FP 3.32-3.33
  Hover button, FP 3.24-3.25
  hyperlinks, FP 3.14-3.15
  marquees, FP 3.26-3.27
  new folders, FP 1.11
  new Web pages, FP 2.2-2.3
  push buttons, FP 3.34-3.35
  Tables, FP 3.6-3.7
  Web sites, FP 2.21-2.24
Custom themes, FP 3.12-3.13
Customer Support Web, FP 2.4
Customer Support Web Wizard, FP 2.8
Cut, FP 4.16-4.17

D

Data Access pages, FP 2.8
Discussion Web Wizard, FP 2.8
Drop-down menu, FP 3.32-3.33

E

Editing, FP 2.14-2.15
  hyperlinks, FP 3.16-3.17
Excel, FP 4.14
Exiting FrontPage, FP 1.16-1.17
Exploring the FrontPage screen, FP 1.6-1.7

F

File:
  open, FP 1.8-1.9
  recent, FP 1.8
File menu, FP 1.8-1.9
Find command, FP 2.16-2.17
Folder List, FP 4.2-4.3, 4.9
Folders view, FP 4.8-4.9
Font, FP 3.2-3.3
Form page, FP 3.28-3.35
Form Properties, FP 3.34-3.35
Formatting:
  images, FP 3.20-3.21
  lists, FP 3.4-3.5
  tables, FP 3.8-3.9
  text, FP 3.2-3.3
  Web pages, FP 3.1-3.41
Formatting toolbar, FP 3.2-3.3
FrontPage:
  exiting, FP 1.16-1.17
  exploring the screen, FP 1.6-1.7
  help, FP 1.14-1.15
  starting, FP 1.4-1.5

G

Graphic Interchange Format (GIF), FP 3.18
Guest Book page, FP 2.2-2.3

H

Help, FP 1.14-1.15
Home page, FP 2.4
Hotspot, FP 3.22-3.23
Hover button, FP 3.24-3.25
HTML, FP 4.14-4.15, 4.16
HTML tab, FP 1.12-1.13

Hyperlinks: FP 1.2,
    creating, FP 3.14-3.15
    editing, FP 3.16-3.17
    verifying, FP 4.10-4.11
Hyperlinks view, FP 4.10-4.11
Hypertext Markup Language,
    FP 1.12

I

I-beam, FP 2.12-2.13
Image mapping, FP 3.22-3.23
Image toolbar, FP 3.20-3.32
Images:
    adding, FP 3.18-3.19
    formatting, FP 3.20
    mapping, FP 3,22-3.23
Import Web Wizard, FP 2.8,
    2.10-2.11
Index, FP 1.14-1.15
Insertion point, FP 2.12-2.13
Internet, FP 1.2
Introduction:
    to Web design software, FP
    1.1
    to Web site design, FP 1.1-
    1.22
Italic, FP 3.2

J

Java, FP 3.24-3.25
Java applet, FP 3.24-3.25
Joint Photographic Experts
    Group (JPEG), FP 3.18

K

Keywords, FP 1.14-1.15

L

List item properties, FP 3.5
Lists, adding and formatting,
    FP 3.4-3.5
Lotus 1-2-3, FP 4.14

M

Maintaining, and publishing
    Web pages, FP 4.1-4.24
Marquee, FP 3.26-3.27
Maximize button, FP 1.6-1.7
Menu bar, FP 1.6-1.7
Microsoft Excel, FP 4.14
Microsoft Word, FP 4.14-4.15
Minimize button, FP 1.6-1.7
Modify Theme, FP 3.12-3.13

N

Navigation bar, FP 4.4-4.5
Navigation view, FP 4.2-4.3
New Page, FP 2.2-2.3
New Web, FP 2.4-2.5
Normal tab, FP 1.12-1.13
Numbered lists, FP 3.4

O

Objects, adding to Web pages,
    FP 3.1-3.41
Office Clipboard, FP 4.1,
    4.16-4.17
Office document, opening in a
    Web, FP 4.14-4.15
Open:
    file, FP 1.8-1.9
    office document, FP 4.14-
    4.15
    Web, FP 1.8
Opening a Web page, FP 1.8-
    1.9

Organizing files in Folders
    view, FP 4.8-4.9

P

Page View, FP 1.12-1.13
Parent page, FP 4.4-4.5
Paste, FP 4.16-4.17
Paste Special, FP 4.16-4.17
Personal Web, FP 2.4
Plain text (TXT or ASC II),
    FP 4.14
Preview, FP 1.12-1.13
Preview a Web page in a
    browser, FP 2.18-2.19
Print Preview, FP 4.6-4.7
Printing the Web structure, FP
    4.6
Project Web, FP 2.4
Properties, FP 4.7
Publishing a Web, FP 4.18-
    4.19
Publishing and Manitaining
    Web Pages, FP 4.1-4.24
Push button, FP 3.34-3.35

R

Radio buttons, FP 3.30-3.31
Recalculate hyperlinks, FP
    4.10
Rename, FP 4.8-4.9, 4.12-
    4.13
Replace, FP 2.16-2.17
Reports view, FP 4.10-4.11
Resizing arrows, FP 3.8
Restore button, FP 1.6-1.7
Rich Text Format (RTF), FP
    4.14
Rows, FP 3.8

S

Save command, FP 1.10
Save embedded files, FP 3.20

Save file, FP 1.18
Saving:
   a Web page, FP 1.10-1.11
Scroll arrows, FP 2.2-2.3
Scroll bars, FP 2.2-2.3
Shared borders, FP 4.4-4.5
Site Summary, FP 4.10-4.11
Sizing buttons, FP 1.6-1.7
Sizing handles, FP 3.20
Spell checking, FP 2.14-2.15
Standard toolbar, FP 1.6-1.7
Start menu, FP 1.4-1.5
Starting FrontPage, FP 1.4-1.5
Status bar, FP 1.6-1.7

T

Tables:
   creating, FP 3.6-3.7
   formatting, FP 3.8-3.9
Target address, FP 3.15
Taskbar, windows, FP 1.4-1.5
Template, FP 2.2, 2.4-2.5
Text:
   adding to a Web page, FP 2.12-2.13
   formatting, FP 3.2-3.3
Text boxes, FP 3.28-3.29
Themes:
   applying, FP 3.10-3.11
   custom themes, FP 3.12-3.13
Title bar, FP 1.6-1.7
Toolbar:
   formatting, FP 3.2-3.3
   image, FP 3.20-3.23
   standard, FP 1.6-1.7
Tree diagram, FP 4.2-4.3

U

Underline, FP 3.2-3.3
Uniform Resource Location (URL), FP 1.2, 3.14-3.15, 4.12-4.13

V

Verifying hyperlinks, FP 4.10-4.11
View:
   folders, FP 1.6-1.7, 4.8-4.9
   hyperlinks, FP 1.6-1.7, 4.10-4.11
   navigation, FP 1.6-1.7, 4.2-4.3, 4.4-4.5
   page, FP 1.6-1.7
   reports, FP 1.6-1.7, 4.10-4.11
   tasks, FP 1.6-1.7
View buttons, FP 1.6-1.7
Viewing and printing the Web structure, FP 4.6-4.7
Views bar, FP 1.6-1.7

W

Web:
   applying themes to, FP 3.10-3.11
   defined, FP 1.6-1.7
   hierarchy, FP 4.2-4.3
   new, FP 2.4-2.5
   open, FP 1.8
   publishing, FP 4.18-4.19
   recent, FP 1.8
   server, FP 2.5, 4.18-4.19
   viewing and printing the structure of, FP 4.6-4.7
   Wizard, FP 2.6-2.9
Web Browser, FP 1.8, 2.18-2.19, 3.24
Web Design Software, introduction to, FP 1.2-1.3
Web hierarchy, FP 4.2-4.3
Web Pages:
   adding objects to, FP 3.1-3.41
   adding text to, FP 2.12-2.13
   creating new, FP 2.2-2.3
   defined, FP 1.2
   editing, FP 2.14-2.15
   formatting, FP 3.1-3.41
   opening, FP 1.8-1.9
   previewing in browser, FP 2.18-2.19
   publishing and maintaining, FP 4.1-4.24
   renaming, FP 4.12-4.13
   saving, FP 1.10-1.11
   spell checking, FP 2.14-2.15
Web Sites: FP 1.1
   creating, FP 2.1-2.24
   defined, FP 1.2
   design, introduction to, FP 1.1-1.22
What's this, FP 1.14
Windows:
   taskbar, FP 1.4-1.5
Wizard:
   Form Page, FP 3.31
   Import Web, FP 2.10-2.11
   Web, FP 2.6-2.9
Word, FP 4.14-4.15
WordPerfect, FP 4.14
Works, FP 4.14

Notes • Notes

Notes • Notes

Notes • Notes